# A Shepherd in Their Midst

## The Episcopacy of Girolamo Seripando (1554-1563)

Augustinian Novitiate
Racine, WI 53402

THE AUGUSTINIAN SERIES
VOLUME 21

# A Shepherd in Their Midst

## The Episcopacy of Girolamo Seripando (1554–1563)

Francesco C. Cesareo

With a Foreword by
John C. Olin

Augustinian Press
1999

*Library of Congress Cataloging-in-Publication Data*

Cesareo, Francesco C., 1959-
    A shepherd in their midst : the episcopacy of Girolamo Seripando (1554-1563) / Francesco C. Cesareo ; with a foreword by John C. Olin.
      p. cm. — (The Augustinian series ; v. 21)
    Includes bibliographical references and index.
    ISBN 1-889542-08-3 (pbk.)
    1. Seripando, Girolamo, 1493-1563. 2. Catholic Church. Archdiocese of Salerno (Italy) — History. 3. Salerno Region (Italy) — Church history. I. Title. II. Series.
Bx4705.S54C47   1999
282'.092—dc21
[B]                                                      98-49786
                                                                          CIP

# DEDICATION

*To my wife Filomena
in gratitude for her
support and encouragement*

# Contents

Foreword . . . . . . . . . . . . . . . . . . . . . . . . . . . . 9
Preface . . . . . . . . . . . . . . . . . . . . . . . . . . . . . 13
Abbreviations . . . . . . . . . . . . . . . . . . . . . . . . . 17
Chapter One: Biographical Sketch . . . . . . . . . . . 19
Chapter Two: The Intellectual and Political World
    of Girolamo Seripando . . . . . . . . . . . . . . . 47
Chapter Three: The Image of Bishop in Seripando's
    Thought . . . . . . . . . . . . . . . . . . . . . . . . 69
Chapter Four: The Spiritual Teachings in the
    Sermons of Girolamo Seripando . . . . . . . . 89
Chapter Five: The Reforms in Salerno . . . . . . . . 125
Chapter Six: Conclusion . . . . . . . . . . . . . . . . 155
A Selected Bibliography . . . . . . . . . . . . . . . . 159

# FOREWORD

In discussing Catholic reform some time ago I wrote that "singular circumstances and demands confronted the Church at the turn of the sixteenth century and that an extraordinary era of religious ferment, activity, and reform now began." The Protestant Reformation soon took place, but I was thinking of other reform efforts whose origins were prior to Luther's and which were independent of the Protestant movements and which remained within the ambit of the Catholic Church. I proceeded to enumerate and describe a number of those, beginning with Savonarola and Cardinal Ximenes at the end of the fifteenth century. My account, I felt, indicated a coherent movement within the Church which could be called Catholic Reform (with a capital R) or even the Catholic Reformation. I believed those terms expressed a valid conceptualization, though I did not mean to use them in too narrow or rigid a sense. I also thought it was important from an historical point of view to tell the story of reform and renewal activities within the Catholic Church. In the aftermath of the Protestant Reformation they had not always been given their due.

The study of Girolamo Seripando that we have before us fits perfectly into that picture. He is a representative *par excellence* of Catholic Reform. He had a long and outstanding career in the Church — Augustinian friar, scholar and preacher of note, prior general of the Augustinians, archbishop of Salerno, active participant in the Council of Trent, cardinal — and in every capacity he sought the goals and embodied the ideals of that movement. Professor Cesareo focuses his study on Seripando's role as archbishop of Salerno, a post he occupied from 1554 to his death in 1563, and on all he did to restore and reform that diocese and revive its spiritual life. He was preeminently the pastor and teacher of those entrusted to his care, and Professor Cesareo gives special attention to his sermons, the effective instrument in fulfilling that responsibility. First and foremost, however, it should be stressed, he resided in his see, an action which at least in this instance corrected one of the worst abuses in the Church at this time. Non-residence was widespread, almost the norm. It was "the calamity of our age" in the words of another Catholic reformer, and from it flowed a host of other ills. In this and every other respect Seripando harks back to an earlier and better kind of bishop and was a model and an influence that the Church in the sixteenth century sorely needed.

There is more however to the role of Seripando as Catholic reformer than his exemplary work as archbishop of Salerno. Professor Cesareo, of course, is well aware of this and discusses Seripando's background and earlier career in his opening chapters. Let me nevertheless call attention to two key features of that background which by extension are also integral aspects of the whole movement of Catholic Reform in the sixteenth century. One is that Seripando was a member and a product of a reformed and more observant Augustinian congregation and from his entry into the Order in 1507 was the disciple and protégé of a truly outstanding prior general Giles of Viterbo. The other is that he was educated in the humanism of the Renaissance and here again Giles of Viterbo was an influence and a guide.

The sixteenth century saw the formation of many new religious Orders in the Church, signs of a religious awakening as well as instruments of more general religious reform. It also witnessed a reform of older Orders, that is, movements for a stricter observance of the original rules of those Orders. This kind of reform was not uncommon in the later middle ages, but in the sixteenth century it can be linked to the broader movement of Catholic Reform. In short the reformed and observant older Orders like the new ones were seedbeds for that broader movement of reform. Giles of Viterbo and Seripando exemplify this in the case of the Augustinians, as indeed does Saint Thomas of Villanova, later archbishop of Valencia, in Spain. I might also note that Martin Luther at that time belonged to an observant Augustinian congregation in Germany and in fact came to Rome in 1510 in connection with Giles of Viterbo's plan for reform in the Saxon province. One wonders if the German friar on this occasion met his prior general!

The link between humanist scholarship and learning and religious reform in this era is equally an important and fruitful relationship. Humanism in this context refers to the intense interest in and study of the ancient classics and it embraced as well the closer study of holy scripture and the early Fathers. This going back to the sources of Europe's culture and faith — *ad fontes* was the battle cry — created the ferment, generated the impetus, and set standards and goals for reform. We can say it was the intellectual background for the Reformation, Protestant as well as Catholic, and it is of major importance in the story of Giles of Viterbo and Girolamo Seripando and of many others who gave life and meaning to the movement of Catholic Reform.

John C. Olin
Professor Emeritus
Fordham University

# PREFACE

Girolamo Seripando lived between 1493-1563, a critical period in the history of the Roman Catholic Church. These were years which saw the need for urgent reform, the spread of Protestantism, the disintegration of religious life, and preparations for a General Council. In light of this, Girolamo Seripando is often portrayed as one of the most eminent figures of pre-Tridentine and Tridentine reform. Historians of the sixteenth century have remembered him as a humanist theologian, reformer of the Augustinian Order, archbishop of Salerno, and legate at the Council of Trent.

In each of these areas, Seripando made significant contributions toward the renewal of the Church. Curiously, however, his brief reign as archbishop of Salerno, which spanned the years 1554 to 1563, has received little attention among scholars. While in recent years Italian historians have begun to show interest in Seripando's episcopacy, there are no works in English which study these important years. In fact, the only book-length work in English on Seripando is the translation of Hubert Jedin's exhaustive study of him, which primarily focuses on his efforts as a legate at the Council of Trent. The neglect of Seripando's episcopacy has, I believe, left a void in Catholic Reformation studies. This work attempts to fill that void by focusing exclusively on Seripando's years as archbishop of Salerno.

Girolamo Seripando believed that the office of bishop needed to be restored if a general reform of the Church, clergy, and faithful was to be accomplished. What was the nature of this restoration? In order to answer this question, this study will examine Seripando's understanding of the episcopal office and the way he embodied this understanding in the governance of Salerno. In particular, this work will demonstrate how Seripando revived the patristic image of the bishop as pastor and teacher, which set him apart from the majority of the bishops of the sixteenth century, thereby foreshadowing the Tridentine-type bishop that would emerge after the Council of Trent. Residing in his diocese, an uncommon practice at the time, Seripando embarked on a reform program that sought to renew the spiritual life of Salerno and correct the abuses that plagued the faithful and the clergy. An integral part of this reform program was the sermon. Particular attention will be given to an analysis of Seripando's sermons, examining to what extent the spirituality embodied therein was Augustinian in nature as he sought to initiate a meaningful reform of the diocese. It is my hope that the significance of Seripando's episcopacy and its importance to the Catholic reform movement will be apparent through this study.

In order to accomplish these aims, this study will approach Seripando's episcopacy thematically. To provide a context for the proper understanding of the place Seripando's episcopacy holds in his vast ecclesiastical career, the first chapter will present a biographical sketch of his life and career. The second chapter will examine the influences on Seripando's thought and spirituality, emphasizing the teachings of Saint Augustine, Neoplatonism, Renaissance humanism, and the Augustinian spiritual tradition. This chapter will also explore the political, economic, and religious climate in Salerno at the time of Seripando's appointment. An examination of the image of bishop in Seripando's thought will be the focus of the third chapter. An in-depth analysis of the spiritual teachings found in Seripando's sermons will be the focus of the fourth chapter, highlighting the link between the spirituality expressed in the sermons and his desire to initiate an inner renewal in the lives of the faithful. The final chapter will examine the various reform measures Seripando enacted in the diocese. The study ends with a brief assessment of his episcopacy.

I have spent several years working on this project and am indebted to many people and institutions for their assistance and encouragement. Special thanks go to John C. Olin, John McManamon, S.J., and Joseph F. Kelly for taking the time to read the manuscript and offer useful comments and criticisms for improving the text. My gratitude to Donald Poduska for his assistance with the translation of the Latin texts and to Sally Joranko for her assistance with literary style. I wish to thank Fr. John E. Rotelle, O.S.A., director of Augustinian Press, for first inviting me to participate in the Augustinian Heritage Series. He has been most helpful in procuring materials and in the preparation of this manuscript. His patience and understanding in seeing this project come to a completion has been most appreciated. I am especially indebted to the librarians and staffs of the Biblioteca Apostolica Vaticana, the Archivio Segreto Vaticana, the Biblioteca Statale Angelica in Rome, the Augustinian Historical Institute in Rome, the Institutum Patristicum in Rome, and the Biblioteca Nazionale di Napoli, who allowed me access to their holdings and archives. A special word of thanks to Caron Knapp, Interlibrary Loan Librarian at John Carroll University for her assistance in getting books and articles from across the country. I was fortunate to receive a Summer Research Fellowship and a George Grauel Faculty Fellowship from John Carroll University which provided me with the time and resources to travel to Italy and complete this manuscript. I am most grateful to John Carroll University for its support and encouragement of research.

This project coincided with several significant life changes — marriage and the birth of two children. I wish to express my heartfelt thanks to my children, Marianna and Gianfranco. Their curiosity with the world around them and their playful dispositions kept me and this project in their proper perspective, reminding me of what was truly important in life. Last, but certainly not least, to my wife Filomena who has supported and encouraged me through the various stages of this project. Her patience with me and her willingness to sacrifice our time for this study has been most appreciated. For her love, encouragement, and support I am truly grateful and it is to her that I lovingly dedicate this work.

Francesco C. Cesareo
24 June 1997

# ABBREVIATIONS

BAV     Biblioteca Apostolica Vaticana, Rome.

BNN     Biblioteca Nazionale Vittorio Emmanuele III, Naples.

CS     "Costituzioni Sinodali." *Memorie per servire alla storia della Chiesa Salernitana*, 4 vols. Ed. Giuseppe Paesano. Salerno: Raffaello Migliaccio, 1846-1857.

CT     *Concilium Tridentinum. Diariorum, actorum, epistolarum, tractatum nova collectio.* 13 vols. Ed. Societas Goerresiana. Freiburg: Herder, 1901-1938.

Diarium     Gutiérrez, David. "Hieronymi Seripandi 'Diarium de Vita Sua' (1513-1562)." *Analecta Augustiniana* 26 (1963): 5-193.

PRS     Seripando, Girolamo. "Prediche Salernitane." *Girolamo Seripando tra Evangelismo e Riforma Cattolica.* Rocchina M. Abbondanza. Naples: Ferraro, 1982.

PS     *Prediche di Girolamo Seripando Arcivescovo di Salerno.* Ed. Francesco Linguiti. Salerno: Raffaelo Migliaccio, 1858.

## CHAPTER ONE

## BIOGRAPHICAL SKETCH

"You increase the honor of the Roman Church by the greatness of your merits."[1] With these words expressed by Pope Julius III in a papal brief issued on 15 August 1554, the pope praised Girolamo Seripando as he prepared to assume his responsibilities as archbishop of Salerno. Julius III was not alone in such an assessment. Reflecting on Seripando's ecclesiastical career, Tomás de Herrera wrote that he was "a man truly worthy of immortal memory, a lover of reform, one who carried out heavy responsibilities in the religious life and in the Church of God with the greatest honesty and humility, a man who accomplished much and was universally considered capable of even greater things."[2]

While both his contemporaries and later historians have given Seripando a prominent place in the work of Catholic reform as a result of his efforts as prior general of the Augustinians and as a conciliar father and legate at the Council of Trent, his reform program as archbishop of Salerno has been given little attention. This has been partly due to the paucity of documentary sources available surrounding Seripando's episcopal career. Consequently, in her study of Seripando's life, historian Gina Algranati devotes only a few sentences to his pastoral activity in Salerno.[3] In a later study, historian Antonio Fava, writing on Seripando and religious renewal in Salerno, was forced to base his conclusions on the evidence he found in the unedited letters of Seripando housed in the Biblioteca Nazionale in Naples.[4] It is only in Hubert Jedin's monumental study of Seripando that one finds a detailed chapter on Seripando's episcopal career and his pastoral reform program.[5] Despite these limitations, the available writings that coincide with Seripando's episcopacy, in particular his sermons and correspondence, allow us to understand one of the more eminent personalities of both pre-Tridentine and Tridentine Catholic reform.

## EARLY LIFE OF GIROLAMO SERIPANDO

Historians do not agree on the date and place of Girolamo Seripando's birth. Early biographers, in particular Felix Milensius, put his birthplace in Troja in Apulia because of his baptismal name, Trojanus. However, later biographers state that Naples was the city of Seripando's birth, basing this conclusion on two pieces of evidence. First, Seripando's nephew, Marcello, in a dedicatory letter written to Cardinal Marcantonio Amulio in 1567 introducing Seripando's sermons on the Creed, indicates that his uncle was born in Naples.[6] Secondly, these later biographers point out that Seripando himself often referred to Naples as his native city.[7] Modern scholars accept Naples as Seripando's place of birth.

While there is consensus as to where Seripando was born, the date of his birth is more problematic. The traditional date is 6 May 1493. However, Seripando's epitaph states that at his death on 17 March 1563, he was 70 years, 5 months, and 11 days, making 6 October 1492 his date of birth.[8] Given the lack of any conclusive evidence, there remains doubt among historians as to his actual birth date.

There is, however, no doubt that Seripando's family belonged to the Neapolitan *noblesse de robe*. Both his father, Ferrante Seripando, and his mother, Isabella Galeota, were members of the official Neapolitan nobility. This class, which provided the monarchy with officials and bishops, was extremely loyal to the throne and served as the main support of the monarchy against the barons. This branch of the nobility was also characterized by the importance it placed on intellectual development, since the sons of these noble families assumed positions as lawyers and officials in both the state and the church, in contrast to the baronial nobility, who were more concerned with living in luxury and bloody intrigues.[9] Given the importance of intellectual pursuits among the *noblesse de robe*, they came under the influence of Renaissance humanism.

It was in this atmosphere that Seripando and his two brothers and two sisters were raised. When both of his parents died shortly after his birth, Seripando's education was entrusted to his uncle, Francesco Seripando, who ensured that he received the intellectual opportunities characteristic of his class. Seripando's education was clearly humanist in orientation, evidenced by the rapid progress he made in the study of Latin, Greek, and Hebrew.[10] Seripando himself gives us a glimpse into the nature of his studies in his diary, where he states that for six years he had been privileged to receive instruction in literary studies under Ambrogio Patavino.[11]

At the age of fifteen Seripando decided to enter the religious life. He chose to join the Dominicans, entering the monastery of Santa Caterina a Formello. His family, not approving of his decision, forced him to leave the Dominicans, hoping to persuade him to follow a secular career. However, his mind was made up, and once again he sought admittance into a religious order. Convinced of his vocation, his family did not stand in his way. Seripando entered the Augustinian monastery of San Giovanni a Carbonara in Naples, where on 6 May 1507 he received the habit and changed his name from Trojanus to Girolamo.

It was not only his desire for religious life, but also his inclination toward studies, in particular his desire to pursue the *humaniores litterae*, that led to his choice of the Augustinian Order. This ancient monastic order, which in the fifteenth century was privileged with men of great learning and austere piety, preserved and kept alive its traditional love for philosophical and theological studies. In fact, Platonism, which was enjoying a revival because of the humanist emphasis on classical studies, had provoked great interest within many Augustinian monasteries. This interest in Platonism was not merely speculative in nature. The Augustinians viewed this philosophy as a means to deepen their understanding of Saint Augustine's own thought, which had sprung from the comparison of Christian and Neoplatonic doctrine.[12]

In addition to their intellectual tradition, the Augustinians were among the most ardent advocates for the necessity of ecclesiastical reform. Since they fulfilled their priestly ministry through preaching, they saw this as one of the means to initiate the needed reform within the Church. To be effective preachers, the Augustinians had to be well educated. Thus, their preaching ministry was intimately linked with their intellectual tradition. This fusion was a perfect way for Seripando to reconcile his intellectual interests with his faith and desire to live out the precepts of the gospel in service to the Church. It seems that in the Augustinians Seripando had found a religious order most suited to his needs. Giles of Viterbo, the general of the Augustinians, who had come to Naples for the General Chapter in 1507 and who had a reputation for learning and eloquence, recognized immediately the distinguished character of Seripando and endeavored to cultivate his potential by fusing together the fruits of this disposition with the culture of the Augustinians.[13]

## EARLY YEARS IN THE AUGUSTINIAN ORDER

Girolamo Seripando began his studies in the monastery under Master Paul of Genazzano. Given his earlier education, Seripando quickly mastered the rudiments of Greek and dialectics.[14] He also excelled in his studies of philosophy and theology.[15] During the summer of 1510, Giles of Viterbo took Seripando to his residence, where he received additional instruction in Greek.[16] Seripando also accompanied Giles to Rome, where he attended the dialectical exercises provided for students there. He then went to the monastery at Sessa, where he had the opportunity to study the Aristotelian *Organon* for two years.[17] As a result of his intellectual formation, Seripando was able to bring to his explanation of theological doctrines a certain eloquence that was uncommon among his contemporaries. On 17 December 1512 Seripando received permission to be ordained.

These first years in the monastery were ones of study and preparation. Seripando made ample progress, and Giles of Viterbo believed it was time for him to assume a degree of responsibility within the Order. In 1514, the prior general appointed Seripando to the confidential position of scriptor for the Order, and in May of that same year he took charge of the Order's register. Seripando's educational background resulted in his appointment in December 1514 as master of studies in Rome. In this position he lectured on logic, oversaw the lessons of the students, participated in the customary disputations, and made certain that the students recited Matins privately.[18]

All of these responsibilities prevented Seripando from wholeheartedly pursuing his studies. Despite this, the prior general appointed him lector at the Roman house of studies on 12 June

1515. However, he never assumed the duties of this position. Two weeks after his appointment, he went to the monastery of Sant'Agostino in Siena to study theology. It seems that Giles of Viterbo had changed Seripando's plans because of the decline in the conditions of that monastery and his hope that the presence of someone like Seripando in the monastery would foster a reforming spirit within the community. However, Seripando's stay in Siena was cut short when he was sent to Sorrento, where he was to deliver his first series of sermons during the season of Lent. Having completed this assignment, he was transferred to the monastery of San Giacomo in Bologna.[19]

The Bologna period proved more stable for Seripando after the many changes he had experienced in a short period of time. He remained in Bologna for seven years (1516-1523), during which time he continued his studies. Bologna's university still retained its ancient reputation. The students who attended the university came from all over Europe and included such famous individuals as Ulrich von Hutten and Johann Cochlaeus. The eminent theologian Johann Eck delivered a famous disputation on usury at the university. Seripando attended a lecture in philosophy by Pietro Pomponazzo at the university.[20] Besides the university, the various houses of the mendicant orders were centers of theological learning. Among these, the monastery of San Giacomo was highly regarded by the other houses of learning. Under the monastery's regent of studies, Seripando continued his study of theology, while at the same time lecturing the new members in philosophy and theology.[21] In 1518 he was created master of studies with pontifical authority[22] and in 1519 he was made regent of the Bologna college and master of the Order.[23]

It was also during this period that Seripando began to exercise with great efficacy the ministry of preaching in various cities throughout Italy. As previously noted, Seripando delivered his first series of sermons in Sorrento during the Lenten season of 1516. These sermons had attracted much attention among the people, not only for their doctrinal content, but also for their piety.[24] Wherever he preached, the people were captivated not by an empty oratory, but by the profound and accessible message inspired by the gospel.[25] Consequently, he gained the admiration not only of the people of the cities where he preached, but also of the princes as well. In fact, because of his reputation as a preacher, he often delivered sermons before the holy Roman Emperor Charles V, who considered Seripando among the wisest and most useful preachers of the day.[26] Throughout his life, Seripando would remain the true apostolic preacher. The ministry of the word and the work of evangelization would be his lifelong principal activity.

The year 1523 marked the beginning of a new phase in his life marked by successive appointments in the governing of the Augustinian Order. On 21 May of that year he was appointed vicar general of the Congregation of San Giovanni a Carbonara, a position he would hold until 1538. He was also appointed president of the congregational chapter soon to be convened. Seripando's task as vicar general was clear — to reform, correct the customs, and to carry out whatever was necessary "for the welfare of that congregation."[27] Seripando, profoundly spiritual and learned in doctrine, assumed this responsibility working for the moral, spiritual, and disciplinary reform of the community. In order to accomplish this reform he believed two elements were indispensable — observance of the rule of residency and the frequent visitation of the communities entrusted to his care. By visiting these communities, Seripando became personally aware of the reality of the situation within the monastery, as well as the environment the monastery found itself in within a particular city. He also came to know the individual members of the community, learning their concerns and needs. During his visitations, Seripando employed the sermon as a vehicle of reform. His sermons testify to the fact that Seripando had come under the influence of both the humanist movement and Christian Platonism. The sermons he delivered to the communities he visited were not meant for the general populace. The themes he chose and the exposition of those themes reflect his thought and his intellectual tendencies and were thus more suited to a cultivated audience with a humanist orientation.[28] The aim of these sermons remained the fostering of a spirit of renewal and reform within the congregation.

It was during this period as vicar general that Seripando began to come to the attention of those outside the Augustinian Order. Two events in 1534 and 1535 decisively influenced the development of his career. Alessandro Farnese had been elected pope on 13 October 1534. During the first month of his pontificate, Paul III met with Seripando twice in audience.[29] During the Lenten season of 1535, the pope asked that Seripando come to Rome to preach and twice received him in audience. Clearly Paul III was developing confidence in Seripando and planned to utilize his talents when the opportune moment presented itself.

Still more apparent was the distinguished treatment accorded Seripando by the holy Roman Emperor Charles V during his stay in Naples between 1535-1536. During this period, Seripando had several opportunities to preach before the emperor. In addition, it seems that Seripando met with Charles V on various occasions to discuss ecclesiastical reform.[30] These meetings left a favorable impression on the emperor which would manifest itself throughout Seripando's ecclesiastical career.

As Seripando made his way throughout Italy on his visitations or as a preacher, he came into contact with the spirit of the Catholic Reformation. A decisive moment occurred in 1538 when he went to Verona to preach. Because of the efforts of its resident bishop, Gianmatteo Giberti, this city had become the center of ecclesiastical reform and renewed religious life in Italy. Seripando witnessed firsthand the powerful results of a reform-minded bishop who provided both the clergy and the faithful with an example of Christian living. His experience of Giberti would provide Seripando with a model when later in his life he would be called upon to assume the office of bishop. Seripando's stay in Verona also brought him into contact with a new generation of reformers, inspired by the spirit of the Oratory of Divine Love, who believed that the only way the Church could experience a true process of renewal was through self-sanctification and a dedication toward elevating the clergy and working for the salvation of souls.[31]

Seripando's experience of reform in Verona resulted in the employing of his humanist interests and studies in the work of ecclesiastical reform. He also became more concerned with addressing Martin Luther's religious ideas. While Seripando's writings were silent when it came to Luther or any of the other reformers, he had been reading Protestant books. Pope Clement VII in 1531 had granted him permission to read these works. Seripando utilized this permission and carefully studied the writings of the reformers.[32] Yet, even though he was aware of the teachings being developed by the Protestants, his theological essays from this period show no apparent interest in the developing controversy. Remarkably, Seripando treats the central doctrines of the reformers, such as the teaching on justification by faith alone, as if he had never heard of the reformers and their ideas.[33] Nevertheless, it is clear that Seripando had come to know the basic questions of Lutheran theology and that some of Luther's reasoning had made an impression on him. This is evident from the content of his talks after 1538. Whenever he was not obliged to address the practical questions of religious discipline and the common life, he chose such subjects as the justification of the sinner by faith and love, through the merits of Christ.[34]

## YEARS AS PRIOR GENERAL OF THE AUGUSTINIAN ORDER

After fifteen years as vicar general of the Congregation of San Giovanni a Carbonara, Seripando resigned on 23 May 1538. However, a move was already underway to elect him as prior general of the Augustinian Order, indicated by his appointment as president of the general chapter. Two days after the death of the prior general, Giovanni Antonio, Paul III nominated Seripando for the office. The pope believed that he was best suited for the position and best prepared to curtail the inroads of Protestantism within the Augustinians and to carry out a basic reform of the Order.[35] Given the pope's strong backing, he was unanimously elected prior general. Seripando's objections notwithstanding, Paul III confirmed the election at the end of January 1539, charging him with two great tasks — first, the improvement of morals, and second, the preservation of true doctrine.[36]

The years of Seripando's generalate (1539-1551) initiated a new phase in his life. The Church was going through a difficult and delicate period — the necessity and urgency for reform; preparations for an ecumenical council; the diffusion of Lutheran heresy; the moral and disciplinary disintegration of religious orders. During his twelve years as prior general, Seripando zealously labored to preserve the integrity of doctrine, to initiate a general reform of the Augustinians, and to purge the Order of any Lutheran sympathies. To address this last goal, Seripando immediately set to work. At the meeting of the general chapter that had elected him prior general, Seripando reissued an earlier decree that prohibited the members of the Order from possessing or reading Luther's books or from disputing and discussing his teachings. However, cognizant that Luther's theological ideas had for some time penetrated the Order, Seripando recognized the need for more drastic measures. Consequently, a decree was issued by Seripando at the general chapter stating that "all who had been convicted of Lutheranism or had made themselves suspect of it or had given scandal to the people, were to be cast into the monastery prison, deprived of the license to preach, and when their guilt had been determined, they were to be condemned to the galleys."[37] Such a directive was not consistent with Seripando's humanist approach to reform, yet it must be kept in mind that he was a man of his times and such punishment was common in his day.

Despite such prescriptions, Seripando knew that if he was to reform the Order thoroughly, strictness alone would not change individuals. He realized that one has to take people as they are and not allow them to labor under the delusion that they can change with one stroke and move in another direction. One has to win them for the good, lead them to the new form.[38] In an address given in Rome on 21 January 1539, after papal confirmation of his election, Seripando provided a glimpse into his view of the office of prior general. He highlighted the qualities needed by one called to administer a community — first, the will to become father and shepherd to those entrusted to him; second, the prudence in keeping with his office to lead them to virtue; and third, a never tiring energy.[39] Seripando went on to state that the superior is to assist all with his counsel; he is not to esteem anyone lightly; he is to heal the injuries of religious life and restrain within bounds the evil, but must also be willing to listen to every individual and understand.[40]

Underlying this view was Seripando's understanding of reform. *"Reformatio"* meant a reform that returned to the spirit of the founders and was realized in the individual by desecularization, which involved limiting contact with secular society, and the action of grace. On this basic idea the whole practical program of Seripando for the renewal of his Order is founded. The most important points for reform were first, developing the liturgical life of the community; second, fostering peace and love among the members of the community; third, encouraging theological studies; and fourth, providing for the orderly management of temporalities.[41] These ideas were concretized in the reform efforts initiated by Seripando at the general chapter held in Naples in 1539.

From the prior general's perspective, there were several areas that needed to be reformed within the Order. First and foremost was the reestablishment of communal life. Monasticism had declined as a result of the monastery's involvement with outside economic activities. A further consequence of this involvement was the intrusion of a secular spirit within the community. In order to combat this, Seripando highlighted the need for the entire community to gather together for liturgical functions and choir, as well as to deepen their awareness of the spiritual life by means of a strict observance of the Augustinian Rule and of those tasks assigned to each individual for the benefit of the community. Seripando also proposed a renewal of studies as a means of restoring the community to the spirit of its founder.[42] Furthermore, he limited the external pomp surrounding the general chapter, ordering that only those who according to the Order's Constitutions had the right to participate in the general chapter should attend, along with those expressly invited by the prior general. No other members of the Order could attend.[43] It seems that Seripando hoped, with these initial attempts, to attain an internal and external reform of the Order based on the renewal of a profound spiritual life and the restoration of strict discipline.

The reform and renewal of the Order was to be accomplished through the statutes and decrees promulgated by the three general chapters held by Seripando and the hundreds of decrees that were issued. However, this whole legislative work constituted only part, and perhaps not even the most important part, of his activity. The essence of his reform effort was the highly personal influence of the prior general on the members of the Order by word and example. Seripando desired to employ a personal approach, which involved the visitation of the monastic communities of the Order both within and outside of Italy. In order to carry out this style of reform, he petitioned the pope for permission to visit the entire Order.

Having received the pope's permission, Seripando began his journey on 18 November 1539. The visitation would last until 1542 and would take him to the monastic communities in Italy, France, Spain, and Portugal.[44] It would be impossible for Seripando to visit every monastery. Thus, he would visit only the larger communities, together with the smaller houses along the travel route. The visitation was guided by certain fundamental principles that reflect Seripando's desire to implement meaningful reform. The first principle regulated his comportment as prior general during the visit. He was to proceed with a general spirit of openness, conducting each visit with "the eye seeing, the ear hearing, the mind thinking, the heart loving." Secondly, the general must be aware that "he ought to rule over those below not only with authority and power but also with magnanimity and justice." Finally, the true reform should begin with each individual himself, in order for that person to then implement it among the others, understanding that "he know himself first and then judge those souls subject to himself with equal measure."[45] These criteria guided Seripando's pastoral activities throughout the visitations and bestowed a spirit of humaneness and prudence to the reform statutes that he promulgated before he left a monastery. In addition, he was careful to choose capable men to supervise the implementation of these statutes.

For Seripando, his principal duty during the visitations was to work for the religious and moral rebirth of the Order. To accomplish this, he made use of sermons, addresses, and conferences. As a rule, Seripando began his visitations with an address to the community, explaining his understanding of the office of prior general and outlining the objects of reform.[46] The first object of the visitation was to survey the religious, moral, and economic condition of the community. Seripando did this by meeting with each member of the monastery on a one-on-one basis, as well as by speaking with them in an informal manner during dinner and common recreation "because then the monks were more unrestrained in their replies."[47] At the end of the visitation, Seripando issued reform statutes which were meant to assist the monks in the living out of their lifestyle in accordance with the observance of the Rule and Constitutions, as well as the decrees issued by the general chapter. In addition, these remedies were meant to preserve or re-establish a uniformity of Augustinian life throughout the Order.[48]

Seripando supplemented the statutes with sermons, which also reveal the seriousness with which he undertook the task of reform. In general, each sermon began with a text from the scriptures, in which Seripando tried to foster among the listeners a personal and inner relationship with God and Christ. From there, he went on to draw practical implications for life in the monastery.[49] In the sermons, as well as in the addresses and conferences, "the outstanding trait of Seripando's efforts for reform is that he never desired to command but desired rather to convince and persuade men to accept reform and his high ideals."[50]

Seripando repeated this process during the two years visiting the houses of the Order. On 3 April 1542 he arrived in Rome, where he was received on 10 April by Paul III whom he informed of his findings during the visitation. He also submitted to the pope the statutes he had promulgated. Paul III approved the statutes and confirmed the actions and decisions that Seripando had implemented in the various monasteries of the Order he had visited.[51]

The seriousness with which Seripando took his responsibilities as prior general is seen in his continued efforts to visit the houses in Italy after his return in 1542, as well as his supervision of the Order during his participation at the Council of Trent. In the midst of the theological and disciplinary disputes, Seripando did not set aside his efforts to reform the Order. On a regular basis he sent to the monasteries, provincial priors, and visitators letters in which he issued directives, orders, stern reproaches, or advice on various matters.[52] Until the opening of the Council of Trent, Seripando had governed the Augustinians with a firm hand, giving little freedom to the provincial priors in making decisions on matters of importance. During the Council, while out of necessity he gave the provincial priors more freedom, he continued to hold the reins of government firmly in his hands.

While such an approach was autocratic in nature, it had a positive impact on the Order. The Augustinian Order found itself in a far better state in 1551, the year Seripando stepped down as prior general, than it had been in 1539, the year he assumed that office. This improvement without doubt resulted from the tireless efforts of Seripando, who did not cease to preach and to implement the fundamental characteristics of monastic reform — the restoration of the common life, the renewal of adequate spiritual and intellectual formation of the monks, the promotion of worthy individuals to the priesthood, and the restoration of strict observance of the Rule.[53] Paul III's assessment of Seripando as the most suitable man to govern the Augustinians during a critical period in its history was certainly accurate. In Seripando the Order had been entrusted to a scholar, theologian, and, above all, a reformer.

## THE FIRST PERIOD OF THE COUNCIL OF TRENT

After several failed attempts, the Council of Trent, which had been convoked by Paul III in the papal bull *Laetare Jerusalem* (19 November 1544) to meet at Trent on 15 March 1545, finally opened on 13 December 1545. As prior general of the Augustinians, Seripando began making preparations to attend the council shortly after the pope's convocation. On 11 April 1545 he met with the pope and departed Rome for Trent eight days later, arriving in the city on 19 May.[54] Seripando had long been a supporter of a council, and his participation at the council as both a noted theologian and as one knowledgeable about Augustine's teachings was most welcomed by the assembled bishops. Seripando believed that it was not enough for the council merely to combat Lutheran teachings. Rather, from his perspective it was important to oppose Luther's doctrine with a sound spirituality founded on the dogmas of the Church, along with a Catholic interpretation of Saint Paul's teachings and Saint Augustine's writings.[55]

Therefore, in light of the Council of Trent's aim to bring about a general religious and moral renewal within the Church, Seripando contributed to the discussions his ideas, experience, learning, and theological knowledge. Given his background, he was entrusted with two tasks early on. On 5 March 1546 the council charged him to prepare an outline of the errors and deviations being diffused concerning sacred scripture and to formulate clear remedies to be presented before the Council Fathers. His second duty was to assist in formulating a decree against abuses.[56]

Among the earliest issues debated at Trent was the relationship between preachers from religious orders and the local bishop, who sought greater control over the former. As the superior of a religious order that engaged extensively in preaching, Seripando emerged as the principal voice in defense of the rights of religious to preach in their own churches without the consent of the local bishop. Seripando clearly expresses his view in a letter to Francesco Quignones, the Cardinal of Santa Croce:

> However, when the bishops do not want to carry out the duties of their office, that is to preach, they cannot in good conscience ask to be judges of preachers, who were not instituted by them, but by the Apostolic See to ensure that there be preachers in the Church. . . . If the bishops do not want to preach, what kind of judges of preachers can they be over those the pope will ordain to preach in every province? I therefore protest that every time preachers shall be subject to anyone other than the Apostolic See, that See will have lost the most important thing it possesses.[57]

Seripando's intervention made a great impression and was decisive in the long debate over the decree. Ultimately, the council fathers arrived at a compromise that gave the orders almost complete freedom in their own churches, but required them to receive the bishop's license when they preached in other churches.[58]

In conjunction with this debate, Seripando had also been instrumental in the decree, promulgated during the fifth session on 17 June 1546, on the reading of the Bible and on preaching. This decree sought to renew preaching by placing the responsibility for the religious instruction of the faithful, which should rest more firmly on sacred scripture, on bishops and pastors.[59]

The climax of Seripando's activity during this first period of the Council of Trent came during the discussions of original sin and justification. Jedin has extensively analyzed his involvement in these debates and his overall thought on these critical teachings. Thus, here I will limit myself to a brief summary of Seripando's involvement. As Jedin points out, Seripando's "name is inseparable from the story of the decree on original sin and justification. As a silent worker in drafting the decree and by his appearance before the general congregations he had a positive and negative influence on the formation of the decree."[60]

Seripando's understanding of original sin had been summarized in a treatise he wrote between May and June 1546 entitled *De peccato originale*. For him, unlike many of those present at the Council, the remission of original sin was not merely a consequence of baptism, but rather one of faith and baptism.

> The adult's faith in the death and resurrection of Christ is the indispensable requirement for the forgiveness of original sin; this faith is complemented by the reception of baptism. These two means of salvation are not of the same order, for it is baptism that operates in connection with faith. In the baptism of infants the faith of the sponsor substitutes in a certain manner for the child's faith, which does not exist as yet. But in every case faith is necessary in order that original sin be remitted through application of the grace of redemption and that God may become the father, Christ the brother, and the Holy Spirit the vivifying principle of the moral life of the one baptized.[61]

Seripando based his teaching on original sin on his understanding of concupiscence. Concupiscence is an effect of the moral order, because it impels one toward the transgression of the law and impedes or makes it difficult to observe that law perfectly in this life.[62] In this sense, Seripando understood concupiscence to be called sin, since it is the source of and incitement to many actual sins. As a result, it endangers morality even in the just. Given this view, he petitioned the Council Fathers that the phrase "God hates nothing in the reborn" in the decree on original sin be changed to "so long as God himself heals all our weariness and redeems our life from corruption."[63] The council did not approve his suggestion.

In the discussions surrounding justification, Seripando represented the Augustinian understanding of the doctrine. In the theology of the Augustinians, justification was seen as above all else the work of God, who calls and sustains each individual with his grace. However, they also understood justification as the work of humanity, who must respond to the call of God, and who could with God's help triumph over concupiscence and observe the divine precepts, and with sincere prayer obtain remission of venial sins and an increase in grace in order to progress in virtue.[64] Despite this, the Augustinians insisted that the imperfection, uncertainty, and instability of good works and their merits not be forgotten due to concupiscence.

Seripando's own understanding of justification echoed the basic view espoused by the Augustinians. For him three things are necessary for justification — first, the individual must be moved by God through grace; second, the sinner must move freely toward God; third, the sinner must move freely away from sin. Thus, justification is conceived as a movement proceeding from God and freely accepted by the individual. "This movement is not brought about externally or mechanically, but is evoked when God infuses effective motives into a man and thus draws him to himself."[65] Justification, then, includes both the forgiveness of sins as a consequence of Christ's death and the emergence of a new life as a result of Christ's resurrection. The sinner must experience grief for his sins and must have faith.

The doctrine of justification developed by Seripando was influenced by Saint Augustine, as is evident in a short homily Seripando delivered on Galatians 6:2. Seripando stated, "The law of Christ consists in those things by which all dependence on creatures is removed, and all dependence is on God. These are faith, hope, and love, and these three are so closely connected that the true meaning of the scriptures is lost when they are separated."[66] Seripando clearly stated that the formula "faith justifies" meant that faith in union with love justifies. Such a faith was the only kind that could be called the full faith in the Pauline sense. Charity and faith are so intimately linked that the loss of one leads to the loss of the other.[67] For Seripando, only a faith that contains the roots of hope and love justifies. Except for primal justification, which he understood as exclusively an act of God, a faith that is active in love is required for all types of justification. For the primal justification, he requires a faith that will become active in hope and love, thereby manifesting a readiness for good works.[68] Such notions prompted Seripando to propose that the Council consider the theory of double justification.

Besides the doctrinal debates surrounding justification, the Council was also concerned with disciplinary reform. For many of the conciliar fathers gathered at Trent, the restoration of the episcopacy was the avenue by which the internal renewal of the Church would be accomplished. Advocating the residency of bishops in their dioceses, the reformers at Trent desired to restore the pastoral dimension of the episcopate, emphasizing the duties of bishops to their flocks. One of the principal supporters of this reform, Seripando did not cease to advocate what he considered to be the preliminary condition for pastoral renewal, the obligation of residence for bishops and the personal governance of the diocese by the bishop. He not only supported the obligation of residency, but he was also among the minority who believed that residency be declared a part of divine law (*ius divinum*).[69] In the general congregation of 21 June 1546 Seripando, addressing those who believed that there were legitimate reasons for non-residence, stated "Absolutely no impediment exists that can excuse non-residence."[70] Although the Council rejected the *ius divinum*, the sixth session promulgated a reform decree obligating bishops to reside in their diocese. Clearly Seripando's support of this decree resulted from his experience with Gianmatteo Giberti, bishop of Verona, and the reforms Giberti had implemented in the diocese. He knew firsthand what could be accomplished when a bishop resided with his flock, and he himself would reside in Salerno upon his elevation as archbishop.

Seripando also collaborated on the decree *De sacramentis* and on the canons *De baptismo et confirmatione* promulgated on 3 March 1547. He made a further significant contribution in the discussions on the sacrament of penance. He composed a series of twenty-nine articles regarding the errors of Protestant teaching on penance.[71]

On 11 March 1547 the Council of Trent was transferred to the city of Bologna because of an outbreak of disease that caused many to become ill and some to die. Concerned about his own health, Seripando supported the transfer of the council from the time it had first been proposed. He arrived in Bologna on 26 March, but received permission from the pope to leave the council a little more than a month later so that he could attend the general chapter of the Lombard congregation and the chapter of the entire Order in Recanati.[72]

After spending the summer visiting the monasteries of the Order in Umbria and Lazio, Seripando, at the pope's request, returned to Bologna to participate once again in the work of the council. When he arrived, he found that the proceedings of the council had changed. As he states in a letter written on 18 February 1548 to his friend Augusto Cocciano the debates digressed into useless and superfluous directions. Comparing the proceedings of the council while in Trent to the situation in Bologna, he writes "our congregations, which were actions of doctrine and virtue, are transformed into secret murmurings and lamentations, our processions and divine ceremonies are no longer seen."[73] Seripando reluctantly remained in Bologna in obedience to the pope. He was not only preoccupied by the slow development of the council but also by the problems of the various houses within the Order.

Seripando returned to Rome on 27 September 1548 and was received by the pope on 3 October. He informed Paul III of the serious problems afflicting the Augustinians and of the proceedings of the council in Bologna. Remaining in Rome throughout 1549, he was kept busy by his preaching and his continual contact with the superiors of the various communities throughout the Order.[74]

## THE YEARS IMMEDIATELY FOLLOWING THE COUNCIL

In the midst of all this activity, Seripando's health began to fail. On 3 October 1550 he returned to his native city of Naples. Shortly thereafter he moved to Posilipo, hoping this would improve his health, since this city, with its mild climate and hot springs, had been a center of treatment for various medical conditions since antiquity. With his term as prior general coming to an end, and believing that he was close to death since there was no relief from his illness, Seripando resolved not to accept the generalate should he be elected again. To thwart such an occurrence, he sent his letter of resignation to the general chapter. In April 1551 Seripando signed his resignation and made the last entry in the Order's register. A letter sent to the entire Order reports Seripando's decision:

> With great regret not only among ourselves but of all the fathers of the Order who were present at the recently celebrated general chapter in this monastery, it happened that through letters and messengers the Reverend Father Girolamo Seripando resigned the office of prior general, which he held for twelve years, a master of rare example and worthy of eternal memory. This displeasure at the resignation does not only proceed from the universal benevolence which we all had for him, but from the benefit and usefulness experienced by all within the Order under his governance, which will be remembered forever in the minds of all. And we, and everyone, will always be bound to honor and reverence his Paternity, which has so improved and distinguished the Order with his virtue and prudence and has maintained the good opinion and reputation in which it finds itself.[75]

When Seripando received news that the general chapter had accepted his resignation, he felt a heavy burden lifted from his shoulders.

Having been released from the responsibilities of the generalate, he looked forward to a period of tranquility. However, the holy Roman Emperor had other plans in mind. A few days after the general chapter accepted Seripando's resignation, news reached him that Charles V had nominated him for the position of bishop in the diocese of Aquila. Given the overall state of his health, Seripando quickly decided to refuse the appointment. Writing to the emperor in June 1551, Seripando explained his reasons for not accepting the nomination as bishop. After expressing his gratitude to Charles V for his confidence in him and acknowledging that there was no ministry in the Church as worthy as the office of bishop, Seripando explained that he had resigned as prior general of the Augustinians because of serious illness, believing that death was not too far away. Consequently, he would be unable to assume the office of bishop with its heavy responsibilities and duties. Indeed, Seripando went on to state that even a lesser pastoral office would be too great a burden for him.[76] Furthermore, the raw, blustery climate of Aquila would only contribute to the deterioration of his health. Thus, because of the stern judgment with which God threatened those who deserted their flocks, he would not think of accepting the appointment, knowing he would be unable to fulfill the obligation of residence.[77]

The emperor accepted Seripando's reasons for declining the appointment. He was now free to enjoy the *otium litterarum* that had eluded him for so many years. Seripando spent his days in devotion to his studies and preparing for death. It was during this period that he completed a project of significance for the advancement of learning. On 8 July 1552 Pope Julius III issued a brief approving the library Seripando had founded at San Giovanni a Carbonara.[78] Two years earlier he had entered into an agreement with the vicar of the congregation and the prior of the monastery whereby he pledged 500 ducats to establish a public library which would house his own books as well. The monastery agreed to erect a building for the library and assume the responsibility of administering it. By the spring of 1552, the erection and furnishing of the library were complete.[79]

Seripando's "seclusion" from the world was interrupted in March 1553, when he accepted the mission of ambassador to the imperial court on behalf of the Neapolitan nobility who sought the emperor's acknowledgement and the restoration of their privileges regarding local autonomy, which had been ignored and disregarded by the viceroy Pietro di Toledo. The choice of Seripando is not surprising. Not only did he enjoy the emperor's favor, but he himself was of noble background and could therefore represent their interests with confidence.[80] Seripando's mission was circumscribed by an instruction issued on 13 April 1553 that contained thirty-one points. This document highlighted abuses in the administration of justice and civil administration, listed economic demands, requested representation at the imperial court, and called for the re-appointment of those who had been deprived of their offices and pensions. In addition, the nobles sought to limit the powers of the viceroy by securing the regular succession of appeals in the courts and by restoring certain personal rights to land ownership.[81]

On 2 August Seripando was received by Charles V to discuss the issues and concerns he had brought on behalf of the Neapolitan nobility. Several months later, a decree drafted by the counsel of the imperial court that confirmed the privileges and immunities of the nobility was approved by Charles V.[82] On 3 June 1554 Seripando returned to Naples and informed the nobility of the positive outcome of his mission.

## APPOINTMENT AS ARCHBISHOP OF SALERNO

During his mission at the imperial court, a series of events unfolded that would thrust new responsibilities on Seripando's shoulders. On 12 August 1553 Ludovico Torres, the archbishop of Salerno, died. With his death, the nobles of Naples drew up a resolution requesting Charles V to entrust the diocese of Salerno to Seripando. Cardinal Pacheco, who had come to know Seripando during the first period of the Council of Trent, had a similar idea and personally recommended Seripando to the holy Roman Emperor. On 29 October 1553 the emperor's chancellor, Granvella, announced that Charles V had nominated Seripando to be the new archbishop of Salerno, evidence of the emperor's high regard for him. Upon receiving the news, Seripando asked for time to consider the nomination. Two years earlier he had refused the see of Aquila due to serious illness; however, that was no longer a problem. In fact, Seripando's health had improved. The only excuse he could offer for not accepting this appointment was his desire for solitude, although he realized this was not acceptable. As a result he accepted the nomination with the condition that it would be pleasing to the pope and the prior general of the Augustinians.[83] On 30 March 1554 Seripando's nomination was confirmed by the pope.[84] A brief issued on 26 April 1554 allowed him to take possession of the diocese, which he desired to govern personally as quickly as possible.[85] Although he was consecrated a bishop in Rome on 15 May 1554, he was unable to take canonical possession of the diocese until September because he did not have enough money to pay the fees associated with his elevation or for the bestowal of the pallium, symbol of his archiepiscopal authority.

During the four-month period between his consecration and possession of the diocese, Seripando was in regular contact with the vicar general of Salerno, preparing his program of reform, which he intended to implement upon his arrival. Believing that he needed to address the abuses among the clergy if he was to succeed in bringing about a general renewal of the diocese, Seripando began drawing up guidelines for a diocesan synod.[86] One week after taking possession of the diocese, he convened the cathedral chapter, announcing his wish to institute reform. On 23 November 1554 he opened a diocesan synod aimed at reforming the church of Salerno, in particular clerical life. Besides the synod, another characteristic of Seripando's reform program was the pastoral visitation, which he announced on 24 October 1557 in a letter to the entire diocese.[87]

During the six-year period that Seripando resided in his diocese, his continual presence and vigilance in implementing the reforms promulgated by the synod, along with the visitations, contributed to the spiritual transformation and renewal of Salerno. The foundation of his pastoral renewal rested on his belief that the bishop should govern his diocese personally, an idea he had fought for at Trent.

Toward the end of December 1560, Pius IV appointed Seripando to the tribunal of the Roman Inquisition, hoping to alter the course of that body. The members of the Inquisition — Carpi, Pacheco, Puteo, Scotti, and Ghislieri — had all been appointed by Paul IV and had inaugurated the severe measures for which the Inquisition had come to be known.[88] Seripando believed that the times necessitated not the use of rigorous methods but rather charity as a means of bringing back into the Church those who had gone astray.[89] It was precisely this outlook that convinced the pope of his usefulness in altering the scope and direction of the Inquisition. However, Seripando was uncertain that he could assert his view with those who for so long had directed the Inquisition's proceedings. Given his doubts, he petitioned the pope to free him from this responsibility. However, he was unsuccessful.[90] Pius IV had appointed Seripando to represent a milder policy within the Inquisition, and he had confidence that his ability as a theologian, along with his moderate views, would accomplish this.

## PAPAL LEGATE AT THE COUNCIL OF TRENT

The favor with which the papacy looked upon Seripando was evidenced by his elevation to the College of Cardinals on 26 February 1561.[91] The bull of elevation highlights his accomplishments in the Augustinian Order and in Salerno, his learning, integrity, and prudence, and expresses the opinion that he would be of great service to the Church during these difficult times.[92] Indeed, he would be called to serve the Church in a significant fashion. On 10 March 1561, Pius IV named Seripando among the five legates that were to supervise the proceedings of the reconvened Council of Trent.[93] Seripando went to Trent as a faithful legate of the pope, sincerely desiring reform and firmly believing that the crisis in the Church could not be resolved through anathemas and inquisitorial proceedings. As he had always maintained as prior general of the Augustinians, as archbishop of Salerno, as a council father during the first period of Trent, and even in his capacity as legate, a fundamental reform was in the best interests of the papacy; conditions in the Church that cried out for reform should not be covered over with silence. Seripando affirmed that the anxieties and exigencies of the Church at that moment required an internal renewal, a more devout and better prepared clergy, and a well-developed program for the *cura animarum*.[94]

When the third period of the Council of Trent opened in 1561, the problem of episcopal residency was addressed almost immediately. Unfortunately, the decree on residency issued during the sixth session of Trent had not markedly improved the situation. Therefore, a proposal to declare the obligation of residence to be of divine law (*ius divinum*) was once again made by Archbishop Guerrero of Granada, with the support of the papal legates, Cardinals Gonzaga and Seripando. Those who advocated the notion of *ius divinum* were now going to insist on the bishop's apostolic mission to his flock and emphasize the essential connection between the episcopal office and the care of souls by transferring the obligation of residence from the purely juridical sphere to the realm of conscience.[95]

Why was this issue of such importance? The number of bishops in Rome at that time makes the critical nature of this question apparent. In the latter half of the 1540s more than eighty bishops were residing in Rome rather than in their dioceses. That number jumped to 113 in 1556 and, on the eve of the third period of Trent, more than seventy bishops were living in Rome away from their dioceses. Similar conditions existed throughout Europe. "In the words of Claude d'Espence, the French court bishops avoided their dioceses as if the places were 'Scythian wildernesses and Arabian deserts.'"[96] In light of these conditions, episcopal residency was certainly the central problem of ecclesiastical restoration.

Since Seripando supported the notion of *ius divinum*, he was given the task of selecting the eighteen articles from the ninety-three presented by the Italian bishops that dealt with the means of promoting the pastoral obligations of bishops in their dioceses. From these, the legates would choose twelve to present before the general congregation. Seripando worked tirelessly to advance the fundamental notion that the preliminary condition for any form of pastoral renewal was the obligation of bishops to reside in their dioceses, which in turn would ensure that bishops personally govern their dioceses.

In the draft of the decree, Seripando outlined his views on the residency problem. Seripando argued that the command to observe residency rested on Christ's commission to the shepherds of his flock and on Paul's words in Acts 20:28, which state that bishops have been placed over the Church by the Holy Spirit to watch over and shepherd the flock. Therefore, the obligation was enjoined by a divine commandment in the strictest sense of the word.[97] Seripando's insistence on the *ius divinum* brought him into conflict with the curialists at the council, led by the third legate, Cardinal Simonetta, who opposed the idea of basing residency on the notion of divine law on the grounds that it compromised papal primacy and threatened papal authority. Furthermore, the entire curial structure, with its system of benefices, exemptions, and appeals, was at stake. Even Pius IV was disturbed by Seripando's insistence. Initially, the pope had no objections to the definition of the divine obligation to reside as long as such a definition did not limit in any way papal authority. However, under Simonetta's influence, Pius changed his opinion as he came to understand the definition as a manifestation of hatred for papal primacy.[98] Consequently, Seripando, who had been held in great esteem by Pius IV, was now seen by him as an enemy of the Holy See and sided with the curialists on this issue.[99] Given the divisive nature of this debate the legates, under papal orders, decided to suspend discussion of the matter for the time being. While Seripando's motivation behind his insistence on the divine obligation of episcopal residency was his desire to effect a meaningful reform of the Church, he had underestimated the volatile nature of such a debate and the potential dangers that would result from the discussion. He had not foreseen his inability to control the powerful forces opposed to this definition.

The council proceeded to a discussion of decrees on the eucharist and the Sacrifice of the Mass. Seripando involved himself in the formulation of the doctrine and canons that dealt with the Sacrifice of the Mass. As the only member of a religious order among the five legates, he played a special role in the reform of the orders and of nuns.

Seripando's draft for a decree on holy orders, probably written in October 1562, gives a glimpse into his view of the papacy. He calls the pope the visible head of the Church, its bishop and shepherd, "by whom the Church is visibly and admirably ruled, guided, directed, and above all preserved in the unity of the true faith." The pope, "so far as jurisdiction is concerned, possesses the fullness of power."[100] Seripando goes on to state that Christ, the invisible head of the Church, wished to give the Church a visible head in the pope, who would be a guarantee of the unity of faith and the good government of the Church.[101]

## CONCLUSION

The importance of Seripando's involvement at the Council of Trent was due to his active participation in the formulation of dogmatic proposals and reform programs. Recognized by all as a pre-eminent theologian, he often composed difficult reports or instructions. The intensity with which he participated in the debates took its toll on him physically and would prevent him from seeing the council reach its conclusion.

Seripando's health began to fail in October 1562, to the point that he was often unable to attend or participate in the sessions of the council. Nevertheless, he was kept abreast of the council's proceedings by the other legates, as well as by the many council fathers and theologians who came to visit him. Despite his illness, until the final day of his life, he continued to offer advice and suggestions on the various issues being discussed before the council.

In the spring of 1563 his health took a turn for the worse. The catarrh that had been troubling him was complicated by a fever. Given his rapid deterioration, on the morning of 10 March Seripando made his final confession and put his affairs in order.[102] His condition took a decided turn for the worse on 14 March, and on the following day he began to prepare himself for death, receiving Holy Communion. On 16 March Seripando requested that he be anointed and on the following day he died.

Throughout his life Seripando had always been concerned with reform. He believed that reform must begin with action. There were already enough reform laws and decrees. What was lacking, according to Seripando, was effective implementation of reform, particularly from the papacy.[103] Like many of the humanists of his day, Seripando believed that the reform of the Church could come only from a pope who began the reform with himself and then imposed it on others without regard.[104] Seripando had put this philosophy into practice in his own life. Both as prior general and as archbishop he had led the reform cause by implementing what he deemed necessary to attain the renewal of the order or the diocese. He tried to do this at the Council of Trent as well, but was often derailed by the many opposing forces that were operative at the council. Seripando had spent his life in service to the Church, always keeping before his eyes the glory of God and the well-being of Christianity.

## NOTES

1. Julius III, *Magnitudo meritorum*, Biblioteca Apostolica Vaticana, R.G. Concili, IV, 222 (1).

2. David Gutiérrez, *The Augustinians from the Protestant Reformation to the Peace of Westphalia, 1518-1648* (Villanova: Augustinian Historical Institute, 1979), 140.

3. Gina Algranati, *Vita di Fra Geronimo Seripando* (Naples: Francesco Perrella, 1923).

4. Alessandro Fava, "La restaurazione cattolica nella Diocesi di Salerno — L'arcivescovo Seripando," *Rassegna Storica Salernitana* 1 (1938) 105-123.

5. Hubert Jedin, *Papal Legate at the Council of Trent, Cardinal Seripando*, trans. Frederic C. Eckhoff (St. Louis: B. Herder Book Co., 1947).

6. Marcello Seripando, "All'illustrissimo e reverendissimo signore Monsignor Marcantonio Amulio della Santa Romana Chiesa," in *Prediche di Girolamo Seripando Arcivescovo di Salerno*, ed. Francesco Linguiti (Salerno: Raffaello Migliaccio, 1858) 39.

7. Jedin, *Papal Legate*, 1.

8. Ibid., 2.

9. Ibid., 3-4.

10. Rocchina M. Abbondanza, *Girolamo Seripando tra Evangelismo e Riforma Cattolica* (Naples: Ferraro, 1982) 11.

11. David Gutiérrez, "Hieronymi Seripandi 'Diarium de Vita Sua' (1513-1562)," *Analecta Augustiniana* 26 (1963): 105.

12. Ernesto Pontieri, "Girolamo Seripando e la città di Salerno sua sede arcivescovile (1554-1563)," *Rassegna Storica Salernitana* 26 (1965) 4.

13. Francesco Linguiti, *Della vita e delle opere di Girolamo Seripando* (Salerno: Raffaello Migliaccio, 1858), 8.

14. Jedin, *Papal Legate*, 8.
15. Abbondanza, 11.
16. Giuseppe Signorelli, *Il Cardinale Egidio da Viterbo: Agostiniano, umanista e riformatore* (Florence: Editrice Fiorentina, 1929) 45.
17. Jedin, *Papal Legate*, 8.
18. Ibid., 9.
19. Ibid., 10.
20. Ibid., 11.
21. Abbondanza, 12.
22. Algranati, 13.
23. Abbondanza, 12.
24. Gina Algranati, *Saggio di una biografia del Cardinale Seripando* (Foggia: Leone, 1911), document 1, 55.
25. Generoso Crisci, *Il cammino della chiesa salernitana nell'opera dei suoi vescovi*, 4 vols. (Naples: Libreria Editrice Redenzione, 1976-1984) 1:505.
26. Algranati, *Saggio*, document 1, 56.
27. Abbondanza, 13.
28. Ibid., 76.
29. Jedin, *Papal Legate*, 19.
30. "Vita del Cardinale Girolamo Seripando uno dei legati del Concilio di Trento scritto a modo di Giornale da lui medesimo," in *Documenti inediti e nuovi lavori letterarii sul Concilio di Trento*, ed. Generoso Calenzio (Rome: Sinimberghi, 1874), 160.
31. Jedin, *Papal Legate*, 22.
32. Ibid., 102.
33. Ibid., 103.
34. Ibid., 71.
35. Benigno A.L. van Luijk, *L'ordine Agostiniano e la Riforma monastica dal cinquecento alla vigilia della rivoluzione francese* (Louvain: Institut Historique Augustinien, 1973), 22.
36. Jedin, *Papal Legate*, 221.
37. Ibid., 221-22.
38. Hubert Jedin, "Seelenleitung und Vollkommenheitsstreben bei Kardinal Seripando," *Sanctus Augustinus Vitae Spiritualis Magister* (Rome: Analecta Augustiniana, 1959), 391.
39. Ibid., 390-391.
40. Ibid., 391.
41. Ibid., 393.
42. van Luijk, 25.
43. Ibid.
44. Abbondanza, 15.
45. Crisci, 1:510-512.
46. David Gutiérrez, *Los Agustinos desde el protestantismo hasta la restauración católica, 1518-1648* (Rome: Institutum Historicum Ordinis Fratrum S. Augustini, 1971), 45.

47. Ibid. See also Jedin, *Papal Legate*, 138.
48. Gutiérrez, *Los Agustinos*, 45.
49. Jedin, *Papal Legate*, 201,
50. Ibid., 138.
51. Abbondanza, 15.
52. van Luijk, 29.
53. Gutiérrez, *Los Agustinos*, 56.
54. Jedin, *Papal Legate*, 171.
55. Abbondanza, 79.
56. *Diarium*, 63-64.
57. Calenzio, 258-59.
58. Jedin presents a detailed analysis of this debate and the many drafts proposed in *Papal Legate*, 301-313.
59. Abbondanza, 79-80.
60. Jedin, *Papal Legate*, 314.
61. Ibid., 315.
62. Gutiérrez, *Los Agustinos*, 184.
63. CT 12: 544-553.
64. Gutiérrez, *Los Agustinos*, 185.
65. Jedin, *Papal Legate*, 76.
66. Ibid., 90.
67. Ibid.
68. Ibid., 96-97.
69. CT 1: 72, 31ff.
70. CT 5: 260, 26-29.
71. CT 5: 962-67; 12: 740-60. See also Crisci, 1: 516.
72. Jedin, *Papal Legate*, 404.
73. BNN, MS COD XIII, AA, vol. 50, f. 6.
74. Abbondanza, 18.
75. Letter of Christopher of Padua to the Congregation of San Giovanni a Carbonara, in Hubert Jedin, *Girolamo Seripando Sein Leben und Denken im Geisteskampf des 16 Jahrhunderts* (Wurzburg: Rita Verlag, 1937), 568-69.
76. BNN, Vind. Lat. 64, f. 12r.
77. Ibid., f. 12v.
78. Jedin, *Papal Legate*, 437.
79. Ibid., 437-38.
80. Ibid., 444.
81. Ibid., 446.
82. Crisci, 1: 521.
83. BNN, MS COD XIII, AA, vol. 48, f. 43.
84. BNN, MS COD XIII, AA, vol. 61, f. 44.
85. BNN, Vind. Lat., 64, f. 17r.
86. Antonio Balducci, *Girolamo Seripando: Arcivescovo di Salerno, 1554-1563* (Cava dei Tirreni: Arti Grafiche di Mauro, 1963), 55.

87. Ibid., 91.
88. Jedin, *Papal Legate*, 547.
89. BAV, Vat. Lat. 6692, f. 23.
90. *Diarium*, 136.
91. *Diarium*, 138.
92. E. Martène and U. Durand, *Veterum scriptorum et monumentorum ecclesiasticorum et dogmaticorum amplissima collectio*, 9 vols. (Paris, 1724-1733), 3: 1309-12.
93. *Diarium*, 139-40.
94. Abbondanza, 20.
95. Jedin, *Papal Legate*, 600.
96. Ibid.
97. Ibid., 598-99.
98. Ibid., 609-611.
99. *Diarium*, 145.
100. CT 9: 42.
101. Ibid.
102. Jedin, *Papal Legate*, 695. Seripando's last will and testament can be found in Jedin, *Girolamo Seripando Sein Leben*, 648.
103. CT 13: 315-16.
104. *Diarium*, 109.

*Chapter Two*

# The Intellectual and Political World of Girolamo Seripando

The Protestant Reformation and the Catholic Reformation share common origins. At the end of the fifteenth century and the beginning of the sixteenth century, the various reform proposals that emerged within the Church produced a religious revival that was both institutional and personal. For the Protestant reformers such proposals called for doctrinal clarifications as well. Some reformers called for individual conversion, while others were more concerned with renewing the structures of the institutional church. Both of these reform aims were inspired by the patristic revival of the late middle ages and the Renaissance. The Protestant Reformation's quest for a purified Christian life was in many ways in continuity with the religious reform movement that predated Martin Luther. So too the Catholic Reformation grew out of a pre-Lutheran quest for renewed devotion, restored religious observance, and reformed diocesan government.[1]

Among the Church Fathers whose writings were frequently consulted both prior to and during the Reformation era was Saint Augustine. With the hopes of those seeking institutional reform in the fifteenth century dashed because of the struggles among conciliar, papal, and political forces, which undermined the efforts of those seeking practical reform, the reformers began to focus on the problem of salvation. "Here Augustine's confessional discussion of personal conversion, his obsession with the doctrines of justification and predestination, proved of compelling attraction."[2] This preoccupation with Augustine's views became more apparent as Protestant writers and reformers focused on the most central problems of the Christian faith — salvation and grace, justification and predestination.

Within the Catholic Reformation, the beginnings of reform at the end of the fifteenth century and the early sixteenth century were associated above all with bishops and with regulars. In both cases the influential model was Saint Augustine. The image of Augustine as a resident bishop countering heretics by force as well as by argument had an obvious appeal for the reformers. Furthermore, the various religious orders that followed versions of the Rule of Saint Augustine included many branches that were attempting to return to a purer observance of the rule at the end of the fifteenth century.[3]

Thus, the late medieval and early modern eras represented an "Augustinian moment" in Western Christendom that saw the emergence of a new reform movement founded on Saint Augustine's thought. During this period, Augustine was often cited by philosophers and theologians as they formulated their reform ideology. More importantly, the monasteries of the Augustinian Order served as the well-spring of this new reform movement inspired by the views of Augustine.

In many ways Girolamo Seripando was both a product and an instrument of this reform movement. From his youth, he had loved study and contemplation. Upon entering the Augustinians he naturally immersed himself in the theological and philosophical teachings of Augustine. This study led him to the study of Plato, a Plato of Christian interpretation, whose realm of ideas was in deepest accord with Seripando's contemplative bent. If one looks at the influences that affected Seripando until 1530, it is clear that he was a Christian Platonist who would become one of the principal humanists of his day. Besides Augustine, theologically he looked to Thomas Aquinas and Giles of Rome.[4] Seripando's Platonism owed a great deal to the influence of Giles of Viterbo and the circle of Neapolitan humanists connected with the Pontian Academy with whom he associated during his time in Naples.[5] It was during these early formative years that Seripando became sensitive to the burning spiritual problems of his day and began to formulate his own religious outlook. To better appreciate his spiritual teachings and reforms as archbishop, it is important to examine the foundations upon which his religious ideas were based and the particular situation in which Salerno found itself upon his elevation to the episcopacy.

## NEOPLATONISM

The Augustinian Order during the fifteenth century was distinguished by men of exceptional learning and piety. The Order kept alive its traditional love for philosophical and theological studies. Consequently Platonism, which was enjoying a revival due to the humanist interest in antiquity, had found a receptive climate within the Augustinian Order. Platonism was studied as a way to penetrate more deeply the thought of Augustine.[6] As a member of the Augustinians, Seripando himself had also become a follower of Neoplatonism. He had read the classical authors extensively and possessed an extraordinary knowledge of the ancient Greek and Roman classics. This interest in the classics deepened during his long residence in Naples, where he entered into the circle of the Pontian Academy. Seripando developed a close relationship with the members of the Academy, who were discussing and studying the ancient classics. It was during this period in Naples that Seripando made most of his humanist contacts and furthered his Platonic and humanist studies. For Seripando, Plato, along with Virgil and Cicero, guided him in the world of the spirit.

Seripando's relation with Renaissance Platonism can best be understood by the references he makes in his writings. The leader and most influential representative of Renaissance Platonism was Marsilio Ficino, who fused together the medieval philosophical and religious heritage with the teachings of Greek Platonism.[7] Seripando often refers to Ficino's *Platonic Theology*, which provided an authoritative summary of Platonist philosophy, "in which the immortality of the soul is emphasized, reasserting to some extent the Thomist position against the Averroists. . . . His emphasis on the inner ascent of the soul towards God through contemplation links him with the mystics, whereas his doctrine of the unity of the world brought about by the soul influenced the natural philosophers of the sixteenth century."[8] Given the many parallels with the works of Ficino found in Seripando's writings, Jedin states that the relation with the Florentine humanist should be made clear. There is no doubt that "Seripando looked at Neoplatonism through Ficino's spectacles, and that Ficino was the chief source of Neoplatonism for Seripando."[9] Seripando's acceptance of the Platonic theory of ideas and of Neoplatonic mysticism could not alienate him from the essential position of Christian theology. He was a sound scholastic and Augustinian, whose theology (which was Biblical, especially Pauline, and Augustinian in nature) was inspired by the Christian Platonism of his day. Neoplatonism assisted Seripando with his conception of biblical revelation along with a better comprehension of the events of biblical revelation. Seripando saw Platonism as a preparation and an avenue to a Pauline Christianity.[10] Seripando's approach in the direction of his diocese and the pastoral care of souls stems from this fusion of Christian Platonism with his theology.

## AUGUSTINIAN SPIRITUALITY

Certain common views found among the spiritual teachers of the Augustinians formed the basis of what can be characterized as an Augustinian spirituality—the primacy of love, the primacy of grace, and the primacy of Jesus Christ. These spiritual concepts are derived from a constant study of scripture. According to the teaching of sacred scripture, Christian perfection consists basically in love (*caritas*). The love given by God and then directed back to God and neighbor grants to all other virtues life and growth.[11]

Even when every trend of Christian spirituality teaches that the spiritual life is rooted on the one side in the grace of God and on the other side has human free cooperation as a prerequisite, still there are characteristic differences in the way in which one or the other is brought about. The Augustinians emphasize the activity of God, whose grace guides and sets in motion human will. The more basic reason why the Augustinians emphatically stressed the necessity of the help of divine grace in the spiritual life lies in their conviction that the Fall severely weakened human powers to know and to will.[12]

In terms of works, the Augustinians often stressed the lack of good works and warned against self-righteousness which praises its works and trusts in its merits. Without denying the merit of good works before God, the Augustinians liked to refer to the teaching of Augustine that "all our good merits are only gifts of God."[13]

Seripando's piety reflected these Augustinian characteristics. It lived out of Paul's teaching on grace and out of the basic idea of Augustine's *Enchiridion*: faith, hope, and love are a sharing in the Triune God.[14] Augustinian too is Seripando's voluntarism. In human life and in his own life Seripando saw the will of God as operative. To get to know God's will, to bring one's life in line with it, to mistrust one's own will to the utmost, was for Seripando Christian perfection.[15] This appears evident in a letter written while he was legate at the Council of Trent to his friend Placito di Sangro:

> When things do not happen according to what I perceive to be good, I am certain that the blessed God wills that they happen according to what seems good in his eyes. That means saying that if they do not run the way humans would like them to, one must acknowledge that they run as God wills. This teaching of mine is well founded, for never have I read that man should rejoice in the works of his hands; rather I have read that a prophet says to God: In the works of your hands I will rejoice.[16]

For Seripando, this reaching out for the will of God and this mistrust of his own wishes and plans became visible at the turning points of his life.

## RENAISSANCE HUMANISM

Seripando's efforts as a reformer were not only inspired by the teachings of Neoplatonism or the spirituality of the Augustinians, but also by the principles of Renaissance humanism. The term "humanism" has its origin in the *studia humanitatis*, a phrase used in the general sense of a liberal or literary education. As the Renaissance developed, the *studia humanitatis* referred to a particular educational program that involved the study of grammar, rhetoric, history, moral philosophy, and poetry chiefly in the context of classical literature and learning.[17] From this standpoint humanism must first be seen as a particular group of studies. As such it provided an alternative to the scholastic curriculum which emphasized logic, natural philosophy, and metaphysics.

Since Latin literature formed the heart of this educational program, the humanist movement was characterized by the development of classical scholarship. As Kristeller has demonstrated, "classical studies in the Renaissance were rarely, if ever, separated from the literary and practical aim of the rhetorician to write and to speak well."[18] This revival of rhetorical culture based upon classical standards led to the rediscovery of many texts of the ancient Latin authors by the humanists. This involved a return to the original purity of the classical languages accomplished through philology and textual criticism.[19] One result of the humanists' desire to have the best Latin language and style serve as the foundation for the renewal of culture was the rise of Ciceronianism. Cicero occupied an important place in the history of Italian humanism since his writings defined the concept of *humanitas*, that is, living as a cultivated member of society.[20] Language played an important role in this ideal, as rhetoric not only expressed *humanitas* but also was identified with it.[21]

As a result of the emphasis placed on classical Latin and also classical Greek literature, humanism was seen by some as a movement hostile to the teachings of Christianity. Some believed that the pagan authors of antiquity were incompatible with Christianity and should not be read by Christians. The humanists, however, did not share this view. Indeed many had religious motives and even sought to employ humanism in the service of the Church, especially in the study and understanding of sacred scripture and the patristic texts.[22] The battle therefore was not against the Church's tradition but against the ignorance of their day and in many cases against the scholastic method of the theologians.[23]

Many humanist scholars explicitly discussed religious or theological problems in all or a good many of their writings. This movement often associated with Erasmus and the northern humanists, though also clearly evident among Italian humanists, is referred to as Christian humanism since it was oriented toward the return *ad fontes* of the Christian Church and toward the removal of abuses that had accumulated over the centuries in the historical development of so vast an ecclesiastical establishment.[24]

The development of this ecclesiastical organization went hand in hand in the high middle ages with the development of scholasticism. Renaissance humanists tended to diverge sharply from scholastic thought, which seemed to them increasingly remote from human experience and human needs.[25] Since scholasticism desired to make all things intelligible to reason, it especially valued logic. Its interest in rational analysis and demonstration reduced the importance of literary studies, and it viewed rhetoric and literary style with suspicion. For the humanists this resulted in a theology that was irrelevant to the problems and needs of Christian living.[26] In their approach to theology the humanists returned to the Christian classics — Latin and Greek patristic texts along with sacred scripture. In theology, Christian humanism accepted the theology of the Church. It did not neglect any of the essential truths of Christianity, but preferred to emphasize "those that are the most comforting and cheering, in a word, the most human, which it further regards as the most divine and, if one may say so, as the most in accord with infinite goodness. Thus, it does not look upon original sin as the central doctrine, but on the redemption."[27] Given this emphasis, the humanists understood the task of the theologian to be the transformation of people's lives.

This understanding of the theologian as moving the Christian to a better way of life was also embodied by humanist preachers, whose purpose was to relate learning to living and doctrine to action. Though revolving around God and his message, the sermon was linked to people's concerns; that is, truths must be made relevant to the lives of the people.

> The sermons were expected to be doctrinally sound and theologically learned. At the same time they were not meant to be academic. The preacher's learning and all his proficiency in the art of oratory were to be directed to the single goal of aiding his listeners in their efforts to master the most important art of all — the art of good and blessed living. *Ars bene beateque vivendi* was Cicero's expression, but it was given a Christian interpretation by the sacred orators of the court. No phrase brings us closer to what humanist theology or rhetorical theology was concerned with. None more sharply distinguishes that theology from the theology of the schools and schoolmen.[28]

Thus, a sharp distinction was drawn between the scholastic doctor, whose aim was to educate the intellect, and the preacher, whose aim was to move the will.[29] In these preachers we see a fusion between humanism and the Christian message.

These strains of reform humanism were developing across Europe, including Italy, in the fifteenth and sixteenth centuries, especially among religious foundations. By the mid-fifteenth century monks and friars began to take an active part in humanist scholarship. They adopted humanist style and method in various areas such as oratory, epistolography, poetry, and treatises dealing with moral or religious problems.[30] In addition, the monks and friars were also interested in classical scholarship, and many of the Greek and Latin scholars of the Renaissance were members of religious orders.[31] These monks applied the methods of humanist scholarship to both biblical and patristic texts. Thus, the presence of humanism inspired many to dedicate themselves to the regeneration of Christendom, which included a return *ad fontes* and the renewal of religious life.

While the religious took an interest in humanism as a vehicle for reform within their order, many saw in humanism the means for a reform of Christian living within society. The *studia humanitatis* were concerned with individual human beings, with their changing thoughts, values, and feelings, and with human interaction in society. Despite the fact that the humanists read the Greek philosophers, they were chiefly inspired by the Latin orators, along with the poets and historians of antiquity. Therefore Renaissance humanism, as this emphasis suggests, had more than formal importance. Promoted on the ground that it was better suited to the needs of the laity and of life in society, humanist education had "profound epistemological and anthropological implications that pointed to an evangelical spirituality significantly different from the more intellectual spirituality of the previous period."[32] The goal of this spirituality was a well-led life in the community at large resulting in the renewal of Christian society. Given this aim, humanist piety reflected a threefold concern: first, a piety that looked to biblical models; secondly, a piety that was oriented to the laity rather than those in religious orders; and finally, a piety that learned from Augustine and was inspired by the gospels that true prayer arises from the inward being, the heart, rather than relying merely on outward ritual.

Humanist spirituality was, then, a lay phenomenon that testified to a growing sense of the dignity of the lay estate. The honor that humanists attributed to the non-intellectual dimensions of the personality implied that the best or most blessed life is not necessarily a life of contemplation. Christian spirituality might find full expression in a lay life of active service to others. The general sense of lay social obligation central to humanist spirituality was given particular urgency and converted into a movement of active reform by the sense, widespread among humanists, that their own time was one of special moral and religious crisis.[33] The rhetorical Christianity of the humanists was directed to the hearts and feelings of human beings rather than to their intellects, and it aimed to promote not the contemplation of holy mysteries but active works of love in the service of one's neighbor.[34]

As one who was immersed in the humanist educational program as a youth, Seripando incorporated many of these characteristics into his reform program in Salerno. With the humanists of his day, he believed that the structures of the ecclesiastical institution would automatically be renewed when they were brought back to their origins. As one who shared the humanist outlook, Seripando believed that in order for the Church to experience a regeneration, it had to return to the spirit of the gospel that animated the Christian communities during the apostolic and patristic eras. This program, often referred to as evangelism, which the humanists advocated called for making the gospel the source of Christian life and the basis for reform proposals.[35]

In his association with the circle of Neapolitan humanists, Seripando came into contact with the various ideas for the renewal of the Church that were being discussed in Naples. This "Neapolitan reform program" was characterized by three basic aims. First, the cultivation of the inner spiritual life, through frequent participation in the sacraments, especially attendance at Mass. Second, ensuring the proper formation of the clergy and providing for the moral and religious education of the people, in particular the youth who would assume leadership positions in society. Finally, to increase and bring up to date charitable works and institutions.[36] Seripando would apply these basic ideas to the various situations he encountered as archbishop of Salerno as he worked to bring about a regeneration of the faith among the people of his diocese. Before we can turn to that program, the conditions within Salerno on the eve of Seripando's appointment need to be examined in order to appreciate his reform efforts.

## SALERNO IN THE SIXTEENTH CENTURY

The population of the city of Salerno in the mid-sixteenth century was between eight and nine thousand, while that of the archdiocese, which incorporated a larger geographical area than the city itself, was between fifty and fifty-five thousand.[37] At the time of Seripando's nomination, not only did a variety of religious problems afflict the archdiocese of Salerno, but the city itself also suffered administratively and economically. The cause of Salerno's political problems stemmed from the fall from power of the prince of Salerno, Ferrante Sanseverino, in 1552. Following a series of conflicts with the viceroy Pietro di Toledo, Sanseverino openly rebelled against the holy Roman Emperor Charles V and placed himself in the service of the emperor's number-one adversary, Henry II, the king of France.[38] The stability and fortunes of Salerno were intimately linked with the presence of Sanseverino, whose rule made the city the apex of a vast feudal framework that remained virtually independent of any sovereign interference. Under Sanseverino, the city of Salerno experienced years of an intense political and cultural life reminiscent of the splendor of the high middle ages.

Ferrante Sanseverino ruled over a feudal structure made up of a vast patrimony of land. The heart of this principality was Salerno, where the commercial and mercantile activities were concentrated, along with those trades practiced by the artisans and those that were the responsibility of the nobility and the middle class. The political, economic, and cultural fortunes of the principality of Sanseverino were entrusted into the hands of these diverse groups.[39] As a result of these economic activities, Salerno became an attractive trade center for numerous native and foreign merchants in the first half of the sixteenth century.[40]

The revenue generated by the economic growth of Salerno contributed to a period of cultural flowering. During the second half of the fifteenth century, the intellectual and cultural climate of Salerno was characterized in particular by studies in law, medicine, philosophy, and theology. It was also at this time that the "new learning" began to penetrate these areas of study. By the early years of the sixteenth century, Salerno had begun to cultivate a tradition of humanist studies which especially flourished under Sanseverino.[41]

In his palace in Salerno, Ferrante Sanseverino, along with his wife, Isabella Villamarino, ensured the survival of the culture characteristic of Renaissance courtly life. Sanseverino was a great patron of learning, who not only supported the humanists already present in Salerno, but also invited to his court leading intellectual figures who represented humanist culture. Sanseverino desired that humanism as an intellectual movement penetrate the nobility of Salerno, many of whom were still tied to the intellectual tradition of the late middle ages, along with the academic leaders of the city and the well-to-do classes within the city and its outskirts.

Sanseverino believed that this outcome would be facilitated by the presence of those who represented the humanist movement at his court.[42] In addition to the court, Sanseverino ensured that humanism and its proponents found a fertile and favorable environment within the educational institutions of the city. As a result of his efforts, the intellectual and cultural life of Salerno flourished during the years of his rule.[43]

One of the consequences of the economic growth and cultural development that occurred in Salerno under Sanseverino was a change in the social structure of the city. During this time a new nobility was created among the mercantile middle class, whose members had prospered in the economic climate of the early sixteenth century. Given their increased wealth, the members of this class were able to purchase lands that had the title of nobility attached to them. Along with the title came those privileges that accompanied that title.[44] However, the traditional nobility, whose ancient privileges and position were based on heredity, resisted the attempts of the new nobility to encroach upon their prestige and the enjoyment of their traditional privileges.[45] This led to conflicts between these two groups that would erupt into open violence with the end of Sanseverino's rule.

Since Salerno had benefitted from the rule of Sanseverino, his departure in 1552 had disastrous consequences for the city. When Seripando assumed the leadership of the diocese, barely two years had passed since the dissolution of Sanseverino's rule. Salerno was in the midst of a full-blown crisis. The city's academic institutions, for which Salerno was famous, were in great difficulty. The school of law had been forced to close, while the school of medicine was struggling to avoid the same fate. The humanists who had frequented the court of Sanseverino were now merely a memory of the past. Commerce, which had been one of the principal economic resources of the city under Sanseverino's rule, began to stagnate as a result of the continuous threat of an impending landing and the sack of the city by the Turks. In fact, this threat was so real that in 1555 and 1556 Seripando had been forced to seek refuge in a Benedictine monastery.[46] These conditions left the civic administration with a large deficit, as a political and economic crisis engulfed the city.

The animosity and conflict that existed among the upper classes was fueled by the conditions in which Salerno found itself, torn by divisions within the ancient nobility and between the new nobility from the merchant class, as well as between the nobility and the general population. These conflicts became so heated that they threatened the public well-being. Sanseverino had been able to diffuse these tensions with his conciliatory actions. However, now the city seemed to be on the brink of a class warfare.[47] Seripando often referred to this situation in his sermons, hoping somehow to diffuse the crisis.

Seripando provides evidence of the economic problems afflicting Salerno in his descriptions of the state of the church and the city upon his arrival. The entrance gates to the city had been reduced to a state of disrepair. As a result of neglect, many public buildings were on the verge of collapse. In the spiritual realm, Seripando indicates that many churches were in a state of ruin, lacking even the bare necessities for the celebration of the sacraments.[48] Seripando, who had visited Salerno during the reign of Sanseverino, was struck by the contrast between what the city once was and the condition in which it now found itself. Realizing that the Salerno he had once known was the result of Sanseverino's patronage, he also was convinced that as the city's archbishop he had to attempt to address the city's problems. Aware that he would be unable to restore Salerno to the splendor it had enjoyed under Sanseverino, since he did not possess the means to do so, he did work to improve conditions within the city.[49] Seripando furthered the economic improvement of the church in Salerno by reducing its expenses and the various taxes and tithes the diocese owed to Rome, to better reflect the revenue the church generated at that time.[50]

In the hopes of assisting the city on its road to recovery, Seripando, in a letter written on 11 March 1557 to his *maestro di casa*, informs him that he had paid in the name of the city 200 ducats to the Magnificent Matteo Dardano and Prospero Coduto. In another instance, Seripando requested that the clergy of the city, including the regulars, make a financial contribution to the university so as to free it from the debts that burdened the institution.[51] Given the financial problems afflicting the city, it was not uncommon to call upon the clergy for economic assistance. In fact, given the constant threat of a Turkish invasion and the need to be militarily prepared to thwart such an incursion, the city often stripped churches of their precious metals to be used as a means of generating revenue, as well as compelling the clergy to make payments for military expenses.[52]

It must be kept in mind that upon Seripando's arrival in Salerno the political, cultural, and even religious changes that had manifested themselves in the preceding years had fragmented the city even more than it had already been, giving rise to a more diverse social situation. The cultural climate, which was characterized less by spiritual values and more by worldly values, along with the formation of a critical spirit and a tendency toward rational thought, had reinforced the possibility of acquiring new values that were neither inherited nor necessarily religious.[53] This led to a search for meaning in these new ways of thinking and new values. Consequently, a lack of balance between a religious life and a secular life emerged in the city. The former showed signs of decline and abandonment, whereas the latter was in full bloom. In this climate, new ideas coming from outside the city had the possibility of taking hold in the minds of the citizens. It should not be surprising, then, that reform ideas that were circulating in Europe, and in Italy as well, should also have penetrated Salerno.[54] In a city with a major university that attracted students and scholars from throughout Europe, the teachings of Martin Luther and other Protestant reformers could not have failed to leave an impact on the city, as well as to provoke changes in the mentality and thought of the people.

Salerno experienced many of the same religious problems that afflicted other cities in southern Italy. In some respects, Salerno was in better shape religiously than many other dioceses.[55] The common problems that Salerno faced included the chaotic administration of ecclesiastical benefices, the lack of discipline among the clergy, the exempt status of religious superiors and abbots, and the absence of pastors from their parishes and the bishop from the diocese.[56] This last problem was in many respects the cause of all the rest. Many abuses crept into the diocese because there was no resident bishop to guide the faithful in the living out of their faith or to provide the clergy with an example of how to minister to the people. In Salerno, as in the rest of Europe, the bishop lived far away from his diocese, often never even stepping foot within the diocese during his episcopacy. Even though the bishops of Salerno prior to Seripando had not resided in the diocese they had taken an unusual interest in the affairs of the diocese. In fact, these bishops ordered their vicars to make pastoral visitations of the diocese to correct any problems that had arisen. However, despite these visitations, the lack of episcopal authority rendered their outcome fruitless.[57]

Upon first glance, the faith life of Salerno in the fifteenth and sixteenth centuries seemed alive and well, as both the clergy and the people continued to be religious. However, upon closer examination, these expressions of religiosity were merely formal expressions of a faith that appeared stagnant. The spiritual and faith life of Salerno at this time remained in a state of inertia because the clergy and faithful were not challenged to incorporate that faith into their daily lives and activities. As a result, the acts of piety that often seemed the expressions of faith reflected superstitious beliefs on the part of the population.[58] This situation accounted for the gap that existed among both the clergy and the faithful between their faith and their way of life. While there were daily public expressions of the city's religious countenance, these pious acts failed to influence the way people behaved and lived out their life. Thus, while on the one hand people and clergy participated in the ceremonial expressions of their faith, on the other hand they engaged in immoral practices and a general laxity in their lifestyles.[59] It was these conditions that prompted Seripando to instruct the faithful personally and to admonish the clergy to preach on a regular basis.

The cultural climate of the court under Sanseverino contributed to the religious void Salerno was experiencing by the mid-sixteenth century. This void in the religious culture of the city needed to be filled, but the clergy, whose influence had diminished, were unable to restore to the heart of this city the spiritual traditions that it had lost.[60] This inability resulted from the overall decline in the formation and lifestyle of the priests of the day. This decay manifested itself in the clergy's neglect of the *cura animarum* and celebration of religious services, as well as the abuses that swarmed in the ecclesiastical organization. Furthermore, the secular lifestyle of many clerics added to the difficulty of rekindling a genuine religious spirit within the hearts of the people and the city itself. In short, the clergy had become lazy in meeting their religious obligations.[61] Seripando was acutely aware of this and strove to address this problem from the outset of his episcopacy.

Besides the abuses among the clergy and the consequent problems which afflicted the church in Salerno, it seems that heretical teachings penetrated the city in the early sixteenth century. Protestantism had penetrated Italy through Venice because of its geographical position and its commercial relations with the cities of Germany. Lutheran ideas spread not only among the upper classes, but also among the general population. Besides Venice, the teachings of Protestantism also entered Italy through Piedmont and Milan.[62] Seripando himself bears witness to Protestantism's penetration into Italy during his visit of the Order's province of Milan, where, as he reports, Luther's doctrine had spread.[63] Further evidence of Protestantism's presence in Italy can be obtained from the Italian archives of the Inquisition which are known to exist that report several thousand trials for so-called Lutheran heresy. "Between 1530 and 1580, the adherents of the Reformation comprised the great majority (around 70%) of those denounced and tried in these ecclesiastical tribunals."[64]

The avenue by which the Protestant message was disseminated was the pulpit. Protagonists of the Reformation in Italy in this era were mostly friars well-trained in theology who had earned a reputation as excellent preachers.[65] Thus, throughout the peninsula, Italy saw the development of different groups and movements that were connected to the Protestant Reformation. The new teachings, often associated with social movements, tailored the doctrinal content to the situation in the region or the city where the preacher lived.[66]

In Naples, the first signs of Protestantism appeared toward the middle of the fourth decade. During the period of his residency in Naples, the holy Roman Emperor, Charles V, issued a decree on 4 February 1536 forbidding association with heretics. In August of that same year, the vicar of the archdiocese of Naples had several individuals who were suspected of heresy arrested. At the same time, the Theatines had been invited to Naples to halt the spread of Protestantism, as Juan de Valdes began his activities in the city.[67] Despite these efforts, along with a decree that attempted to cut off the secret or private circulation of forbidden books, Protestantism's presence continued to be felt in Naples.[68]

The penetration of Protestantism in Naples was not confined to the city itself, but spread throughout the kingdom. The Dominican preacher and theologian Ambrogio Salvio da Bagnoli bears witness to this in a deposition before the archbishop of Naples, Mario Carafa, on 16 July 1568, concerning the presence of heretical teachings and suspected advocates of these teachings in the principality of Salerno during the year 1546. During the Lenten season of that year, Isabella Villamarino invited da Bagnoli, who was a known adversary of preachers suspected of heresy, to preach in Salerno because she was concerned about the advance of heretical teaching within the principality.[69] According to da Bagnoli's testimony, these "new ideas" were being discussed and diffused among all the members of the city — nobles and artisans, the middle class, men and women, even among the cathedral canons. From what da Bagnoli observed, the presence of heretical teachings was not confined to a few educated individuals who had come into contact with these ideas through their reading or communication with someone outside the city. These heterodox theories had penetrated all levels of society. The passion for religious and theological questions had not been limited to those classes with a certain cultural and educational background, but had made its way down to even the lower classes.[70]

Among the doctrines being attacked by these new ideas was the real presence in the eucharist. Da Bagnoli recounts a story to the archbishop of Naples that testifies to the widespread acceptance of this heresy. He states that there were those among the canons of the cathedral who did not believe that the consecrated host was in any way the actual body of Christ, but merely bread. He goes on to indicate that this heresy was even being discussed by common women from their windows. One of these women asked her neighbor if she would like to go to Mass with her. The neighbor responded that it was not necessary to go to Mass because Christ was not present there since the host was merely bread and that she had just made bread at her uncle's house.[71] Given the seriousness of the situation, as revealed by this account, it was not enough for preachers to denounce these new doctrines from the pulpit. More serious measures had to be undertaken to combat the spread of these heretical teachings. Isabella Villamarino, da Bagnoli, and the vicar of the archdiocese of Salerno all agreed that, given the suspicion of heresy within the city, it was time to open an inquisitorial process in Salerno.[72]

It would seem that these heretical teachings were able to penetrate Salerno, by means of printed works and the pulpit,[73] as a result of the contacts between individuals in the city and those from other regions in Italy, especially in the north, who were associated with the court, the educational institutions, and the commercial affairs of the principality.[74] In particular, the university was a natural forum for the reception and exchange of new ideas. Salerno, which was the seat of three university faculties — medicine, philosophy, and law — could not remain alien and inattentive to the new religious and cultural ideas of that era, especially those that were being introduced and discussed in Naples, which had always been the heart and mind of national and foreign thought, as well as a center of cultural diffusion on the peninsula.[75]

These new religious ideas also found a receptive audience in Salerno. For many members of the upper classes who were sympathetic to the reform movement, the new teachings associated with Protestantism provided them with a faith that was more refreshing and more suitable to their needs. For the common people, whose religiosity was still very much alive but in many ways neglected by the ecclesiastical structure, this movement represented a vehicle for change. The new ideas were not only seen as suitable for redeeming religious institutions and individual piety from abuses and corruption, but also as providing an occasion to express their protest against the social and political injustices they had endured.[76] This climate of receptivity arose from the cultural and intellectual atmosphere cultivated by Ferrante Sanseverino at his court. In the fervent intellectual life of the court, the new religious ideas coming from near and far took root, because the desire of so many for reform led them to dream of a religion that was more responsive to the simplicity and sincerity of their faith. As a result of this situation, it was the inquisitor's hypothesis that an intellectual, a lecturer in law, perhaps invited by Sanseverino himself, was responsible for the introduction of heresy into Salerno.[77]

The inquisitorial process of all those suspected of harboring heretical ideas, of which there were many, was held before Isabella Villamarino, da Bagnoli, and the vicar of the archbishop. The process closed with the abjuration of heretical doctrines by all those who had espoused heretical views. These individuals were pardoned precipitously and in secret fearing the intervention of the viceroy Pietro di Toledo, an enemy of Ferrante Sanseverino and his household.[78]

It seems that this inquisitorial process succeeded in extinguishing the flames of heresy in Salerno. As a precaution, Seripando, who arrived as archbishop in 1554, held a synod that same year, which issued one constitution dealing with heresy. It decreed that within nine days of its publication, anyone, regardless of his status, who was infected with Lutheran or any other heresy, or who spoke badly of the sacraments and the authority of the Church, or of anything else pertaining to the Catholic faith, or who possessed heretical books or books suspected of heresy, was to be made known to the archbishop.[79] Such a decree seemed unnecessary, since a year later Seripando declared in a sermon that he was grateful to God and happy that up to that point he had not found any evidence of the presence of another faith, nor had he received any reports of individuals who had spoken against the doctrines of the Catholic faith.[80]

## CONCLUSION

The intellectual and religious influences, along with the conditions in sixteenth-century Salerno, formed the background to understanding the episcopal career of Girolamo Seripando. His spiritual teachings derived from his connection with the humanist movement of the day and the Augustinian tradition from which he emerged. The political, economic, social, cultural, and religious conditions in Salerno impacted the way he viewed his role as bishop and the reform efforts he implemented in the diocese. Despite his anxiety about the state of the Church, he did have hope for its improvement and reform. What was needed was a fundamental reform, founded upon a revival of the religious and spiritual life of the clergy and the faithful, under the personal guidance and leadership of the bishop. This was the program Seripando set out to implement in Salerno as he took on the duties and responsibilities of bishop.

## NOTES

1. A.D. Wright, *The Counter-Reformation: Catholic Europe and the Non-Christian World* (New York: St. Martin's Press, 1982), 3. For a review of recent studies on the nature and character of the Catholic Reformation see William V. Hudon, "Religion and Society in Early Modern Italy — Old Questions, New Insights," *The American Historical Review* 101 (June 1996): 783-804.
2. Ibid., 3-4.
3. Ibid., 186.
4. Hubert Jedin, *Papal Legate at the Council of Trent, Cardinal Seripando*, trans. Frederic C. Eckhoff (St. Louis: B. Herder Book Co., 1947), 69.

5. Ernesto Pontieri, "Girolamo Seripando e la città di Salerno sua sede arcivescovile (1554-1563)," *Rassegna Storica Salernitana* 26 (1965): 3.

6. Ernesto Pontieri, "Figure e aspetti delle riforme cattolica-tridentina in Campania: Girolamo Seripando e Paolo Burali d'Arrezzo a Napoli," *Divagazioni Storiche e Storiografiche*, 2a serie (Naples: Libreria Scientifica, 1971), 285.

7. Paul O. Kristeller, *Renaissance Thought and Its Sources*, ed. Michael Mooney (New York: Columbia University Press, 1979), 58.

8. Ibid.

9. Jedin, 44.

10. Alfredo Marranzini, *Dibattito Lutero Seripando su "Giustizia e Libertà del Cristiano"* (Brescia: Morcelliana, 1981), 70.

11. Adolar Zumkeller, "The Spirituality of the Augustinians," in *Christian Spirituality: High Middle Ages and Reformation*, ed. Jill Raitt (New York: Crossroad, 1987), 65.

12. Ibid., 65.

13. Ibid., 67.

14. Hubert Jedin, "Seelenleitung und Vollkommenheitsstreben bei Kardinal Seripando," *Sanctus Augustinus Vitae Spiritualis Magister* (Rome: Analecta Augustiniana, 1959), 404.

15. Ibid.

16. BNN, MSS COD XIII, AA, vol. 55, f. 88v.

17. Kristeller, 22.

18. Ibid., 25.

19. Charles L. Stinger, *The Renaissance in Rome* (Bloomington: Indiana University Press, 1985), 52.

20. John F. D'Amico, *Renaissance Humanism in Papal Rome: Humanists and Churchmen on the Eve of the Reformation* (Baltimore: The Johns Hopkins University Press, 1983), 124.

21. Ibid.

22. This is one of the themes of Giuseppe Toffanin in his work *Storia dell'Umanesimo dal XIII al XVI secolo*, 2a ed. (Rome: Perella, 1940). Kristeller also makes this point. See *Renaissance Thought*, 70.

23. For an in-depth study of the relationship between humanism and scholasticism see Erika Rummel, *The Humanist-Scholastic Debate in the Renaissance and Reformation* (Cambridge: Harvard University Press, 1995). Rummel indicates that while one can make the generalization that humanists supported classical learning and the scholastics did not, the protagonists themselves did not speak in such unqualified terms. She contends: "The humanists supported classical learning, *acknowledging however* that pagan authors lacked the light of faith; scholastics cautioned against classical learning, *acknowledging however* that pagan wisdom could be adapted to Christian purposes." See 14ff.

24. See John C. Olin's article, "Erasmus and Reform," in his work *Six Essays on Erasmus* (New York: Fordham University Press, 1979), 1-15.

25. Rummel, 11-12.

26. Ibid., 155.

27. Jordan Aumann, *Christian Spirituality in the Catholic Tradition* (San Francisco: Ignatius Press, 1985), 185.

28. John W. O'Malley, *Praise and Blame in Renaissance Rome* (Durham: Duke University Press, 1979), 124.

29. Frederick J. McGinness, *Right Thinking and Sacred Oratory in Counter-Reformation Rome* (Princeton: Princeton University Press, 1995), 48.

30. Paul O. Kristeller, *Medieval Aspects of Renaissance Learning* (Durham: Duke University Press, 1974), 109-111.

31. Ibid., 112.

32. William J. Bouwsma, "The Spirituality of Renaissance Humanism," in *Christian Spirituality: High Middle Ages and Reformation*, ed. Jill Raitt (New York: Crossroad, 1987), 236.

33. Ibid., 240.

34. Ibid.

35. Ernesto Pontieri, "La cultura umanistico-rinascimentale in Italia e la Chiesa Cattolica," *Divagazioni Storiche e Storiografiche*, 2a serie (Naples: Libreria Scientifica, 1971), 170.

36. Ibid., 244-45.

37. Pontieri, "Girolamo Seripando," 8.

38. Michele Miele, "La penetrazione protestante a Salerno verso la metà del Cinquecento secondo un documento dell'Inquisizione," in *Miscellanea Gilles Gerard Meersseman*, 2 vols. (Padua: Editrice Antenore, 1970), 2: 832.

39. Donato Dente, "Vita culturale ed istituzioni scolastiche a Salerno nel Cinquecento: Note e Documenti," in *Salerno e il Principato Citra nell'età moderna (secoli XVI-XIX)*, ed. Francesco Sofia (Naples: Edizioni Scientifiche Italiane, 1987), 826.

40. Maria Antonietta Del Grosso, *Salerno nel Seicento: Nell'Interno di una città, vol. 2, pt. 2: Le Attivita Economiche* (Salerno: Edisud, 1993), 75.

41. Dente, "Vita culturale," 830.

42. Ibid.

43. Miele, 833.

44. Dente, "Vita culturale," 826.

45. Ibid.

46. Rocchina M. Abbondanza, *Girolamo Seripando tra Evangelismo e Riforma Cattolica* (Naples: Ferraro, 1982), 6.

47. Donato Dente, *Salerno nel Seicento: Nell'Interno di una città, vol. 2, pt. 1: Inediti per la Storia Civile e Religiosa* (Salerno: Edisud, 1993), 299.

48. BNN, MSS COD XIII, AA, vol. 54, f. 77.

49. Alessandro Fava, "La restaurazione cattolica nella Diocesi di Salerno — L'arcivescovo di Salerno," *Rassegna Storica Salernitana* 1 (1938): 112.

50. Ibid., 110.

51. Antonio Balducci, *Girolamo Seripando: Arcivescovo di Salerno, 1554-1563* (Cava dei Tirreni: Arti Grafiche di Mauro, 1963), 47.

52. Ibid., 40.

53. Dente, *Inediti per la Storia*, 2:297.

54. Miele, 833-34.

55. Historians have provided a variety of descriptions of the religious situation in Salerno at the time of Seripando's appointment as archbishop. Gina Algranati states that the faithful had been abandoned by the clergy, while Antonio Fava indicates that Seripando found the diocese in a disastrous condition plagued with grave scandals. Hubert Jedin, while acknowledging that there were some serious problems in Salerno, states that in comparison to other dioceses, particularly in Germany, the state of the clergy in Salerno was extraordinarily good. See Fava, 106; Algranati, 47; Jedin, *Papal Legate*, ch. 27.

56. Donato Dente, *Salerno nel Seicento: Nell'Interno di una città, vol. 1: Istituzioni Culturali* (Salerno: Edisud, 1990), 214.

57. Miele, 831-32.

58. Ibid., 831. See also Balducci, 54.

59. Dente, *Inediti per la Storia*, 292-93.

60. Donato Cosimato, *Salerno nel Seicento: Economia e società* (Salerno: Laveglia, 1989), 71.

61. Pontieri, "Girolamo Seripando," 11.

62. See John Martin, *Venice's Hidden Enemies: Italian Heretics in a Renaissance City* (Berkeley: University of California Press, 1993).

63. Jedin, *Papal Legate*, 105.

64. Silvana Seidel Menchi, "Italy," *The Reformation in National Context*, ed. Bob Scribner (Cambridge: Cambridge University Press, 1994), 184.

65. Ibid., 186.

66. Massimo Firpo, *Riforma protestante ed eresie nell'Italia del Cinquecento* (Rome: Laterza, 1993), 48.

67. Jedin, *Papal Legate*, 107.

68. Firpo, 46.

69. Miele, 830. See also Salvatore Caponetto, *La riforma protestante nell'Italia del Cinquecento* (Torino: Claudiana, 1992), 390.

70. Miele, 834.

71. Caponetto, 392.
72. Miele, 830.
73. Menchi, 186.
74. Ibid., 836.
75. Dente, *Inediti per la Storia*, 313.
76. Ibid., 316.
77. Ibid., 317.
78. Caponetto, 392.
79. Costituzioni Sinodali, "Heretici," *Memorie per servire alla storia della chiesa salernitana*, 4 vols. (Salerno: Raffaello Migliaccio, 1846-1847), 4: 422-23.
80. Girolamo Seripando, *Prediche di Girolamo Seripando Arcivescovo di Salerno*, ed. Francesco Linguiti (Salerno: Raffaelo Migliaccio, 1858), 66.

## Chapter Three

---
## The Image of Bishop in Seripando's Thought
---

On 12 August 1553, Ludovico Torres, the archbishop of Salerno, died. Upon learning of the archbishop's death, some of the nobility in Naples thought that Girolamo Seripando would be a suitable candidate for the vacant see and requested that Charles V nominate him for this dignity. Even before the nobility's resolution arrived at the imperial court, Cardinal Pacheco, who had come to know Seripando at the Council of Trent and believed that he possessed outstanding qualifications, recommended that the emperor elevate Seripando to the see of Salerno. On 29 October 1553 the emperor's chancellor, Granvella, announced on behalf of Charles V that Seripando had been nominated to be the new archbishop of Salerno.[1] The nomination testified to the emperor's high esteem for Seripando, who had declined the nomination to the see of Aquila two years earlier. After some thought, and realizing that the conditions which led to his decline of a bishopric earlier no longer existed, Seripando accepted the nomination.

Seripando's nomination as archbishop of Salerno made him the incumbent of the richest and most important see in southern Italy after Naples. The city of Salerno was not unfamiliar to Seripando. In 1529 he had preached the Lenten sermons in the city. As prior general of the Augustinians, he had visited the monastery of Saint Augustine from 25 February to 5 March 1551 and had at that time preached to the city magistrates. The following year he returned to the monastery of Saint Augustine.[2]

While Seripando had accepted the nomination, he had to await papal confirmation, which occurred on 30 March 1554.[3] Upon receiving word that the pope had accepted Charles V's recommendation, Seripando began making plans to free himself as quickly as possible from his current duties and obligations so that he would be able to go to Salerno to govern the diocese personally, as he believed he was obliged to do.[4] On 26 April 1554 a papal brief was issued allowing him to take possession of the diocese. At this time, most bishops in Italy, as well as throughout Europe, took possession of their diocese without ever taking up residence, since their only interest was in collecting the revenues the diocese ensured them.[5] These bishops appointed vicars who regulated the collection of their revenues. This constituted one of the most serious abuses within the Church at the time, one which Seripando had fought so hard against at the Council of Trent.[6] Now he had the opportunity to put into practice his view of the episcopal office and its responsibilities by taking up residence in Salerno, which he had every intention of doing. However, after his consecration as bishop in Rome on 15 May 1554, he had to wait until September to enter Salerno and take canonical possession of the diocese because he did not have enough money to pay for the bestowal of the pallium, symbol of his archiepiscopal authority, or the fees to Rome associated with his elevation.

## THE STATE OF THE EPISCOPACY

For the reformers at the Council of Trent, the restoration of the episcopate, both moral and administrative, was crucial if the Church was to be genuinely renewed. Earlier attempts at enforcing residency had been made by the Fifth Lateran Council (1512-1517) and by Paul IV, who issued decrees against those bishops who neglected to reside in their diocese. However, these attempts failed, and with their failure the spiritual needs of the Church continued to be neglected. A strengthened episcopate was seen as the very heart of the post-Tridentine Church.[7] If this were going to happen, a new attitude was needed among those who selected individuals to present to the pope as candidates for the episcopacy. Even the papacy needed to consider the appointment of bishops in a new light. Bishoprics were not to be viewed as titular honors that were bestowed on individuals as rewards or favors, according to the reformers gathered at Trent, but as pastoral offices with attention given to caring for the spiritual needs of their flock. This could occur only if bishops resided in their dioceses.[8]

The question of residency had been a concern from the outset of the Council of Trent since many believed that a debate on residency would lead to the reform of the episcopate in general.[9] From the perspective of the legates, a decree on the obligation of bishops to reside formed an essential part of any effective reform. A minority of bishops at Trent desired that the obligation of residency be declared part of the divine law; however, many bishops believed that such a definition would undermine papal primacy.[10] The bishops who supported the divine obligation of residency believed such a declaration would lead to effectual reform because it would awaken the consciences of those who neglected this obligation. Among those who supported this view, as mentioned earlier, was Girolamo Seripando, who in a letter written to Cardinal Charles Borromeo on 17 May 1562 states that he had always been of the opinion that *"residentiam esse Juris Divini."*[11]

Seripando believed that proclaiming the law of residence a part of the divine law would eliminate the excuses with which bishops sought to defend their actions. If bishops could be convinced of the spiritual nature of their office, he believed they would overcome the obstacles that prevented them from residing in their dioceses.[12] In the hope of moving the episcopacy in the right direction, Seripando proposed that bishops be obligated to reside for a minimum of nine months per year.[13]

Supporting Seripando was Cardinal Pacheco, who proposed that bishops who did not reside in their diocese be punished with the loss of a portion of their revenues. If this did not provide them with the incentive to reside, they should then be deprived of their diocese.[14] However, Pacheco presented a more effective remedy for the reform of the episcopacy. He suggested that only qualified individuals who promised to observe the law of residence be appointed as bishops by the pope. "Only the abandonment of the unhappy practice of using bishoprics and benefices to endow curial positions and for literary pensions, and a strict observance of the principle that the needs of the diocese must be considered in selecting candidates for the episcopate, would be able to implement the reform of the Church."[15]

Perhaps Pacheco was thinking of Seripando when he made this proposal. At a time when nominations to the episcopacy were merely a means of reward and revenue for the bishop,

Seripando was among a small group of bishops in the sixteenth century to emphasize the pastoral ministry of the bishop. The Council of Trent had yet to promulgate any legislation, yet by his efforts to restore the spirit of the gospel among his people he was already anticipating the conciliar decrees. To do this he introduced in his diocese, prior to the legislation at Trent, a series of norms for the correction of customs among the clergy and the people. His success in this area rested on his residing in the diocese, the first bishop of Salerno to do so in the sixteenth century.

The four bishops that preceded Seripando — Giovanni de Vera (1500-1507), Federico Fregoso (1507-1533), Nicolo Ridolfi (1533-1548), and Ludovico Torres (1548-1553) — were all worthy men who, despite the fact that they did not reside in their diocese, still expressed their concern over diocesan conditions. These bishops recognized the need to initiate meaningful reform, and in some instances authorized their vicars to conduct pastoral visitations as a means of implementing reform.[16] However, despite their intentions their non-residency undermined the chances of any real reform taking root. While the vicars were competent men, they lacked the authority and prestige that the bishops possessed to renew the religious life of the population.[17] Furthermore, non-residency resulted in grave disorders, especially administratively, in the management of the diocese. The episcopal palace, for example, was uninhabitable due to neglect, and when Seripando arrived he could not live there until all repairs were completed. The cathedral itself, like so many other churches throughout the diocese, was in disrepair.[18] Salerno, then, provides a good picture of the spiritual and administrative deterioration that was a typical outcome of non-residency.

The conditions that Seripando found in Salerno upon his arrival were not peculiar to that diocese. Many dioceses were experiencing the same type of neglect, not only in Italy, but throughout Europe. Episcopal appointments, especially to the more important and profitable dioceses, were often reserved for members of the nobility or at least economically and socially prominent individuals. In these cases the bishop accepted the appointment as a means of securing the revenues, power, and prestige that the diocese brought with it for himself and his family, leaving the actual administration of the church in the hands of another, often a relative.[19] These bishops were clearly unconcerned with the spiritual needs of the faithful, causing the deterioration of the diocese. "The more the bishops of the sixteenth century openly neglected their ecclesiastical duties, the more the reform movement pointed out the discrepancy between the episcopal ideal and the actual conditions of the hierarchy."[20] This led many reformers to write treatises on the obligations of a bishop.

One of the most important treatises on the episcopacy was Gasparo Contarini's *De officio episcopi*, written in 1516 for a friend, Pietro Lippomano, who had just been appointed as bishop of Bergamo. Based on patristic ideals, the treatise is divided into two sections. The first section explains the virtues that a good bishop must possess, while the second section illustrates how a bishop should conduct himself and carry out his duties as shepherd of his flock.[21]

Contarini indicates that among the principal duties of a bishop is the instruction of the faithful in Christian principles and divine laws.[22] In order to do this, the bishop must reside in his diocese. Contarini stresses that a good bishop does not hand over the care of the diocese to someone else, nor does he remain away from the diocese for any prolonged period of time. Even if he is called upon by the pope to serve the Church in a special way, he must return to his diocese as soon as he is freed from his special assignment.[23]

Realizing that the bishop depends on his clergy to assist him in the care of his flock, Contarini states that the bishop should know his clergy. To accomplish this, the bishop should summon the clergy to appear before him and should question them on their ministry.[24] This would ensure the bishop of the quality of the clergy ministering to the faithful.

The treatise also chastises bishops for neglecting the duty that belongs properly to their office, namely preaching. Contarini reminds them that the bishops of antiquity "were wont on feast days and sometimes daily to preach to all the people during Mass, whereby they both instructed those ignorant of Christian doctrine and exhorted all marvelously to an upright life."[25] Thus, the treatise urges bishops to fulfill once again this duty to preach and "either proclaim the gospel or develop some theme from holy scripture or moral philosophy for the public good."[26] For Contarini, the bishop must be a perfect man, in order to possess the moral virtues, and a perfect Christian, in order to possess the theological virtues, so that he could carry out the responsibilities of his office, namely, the care of souls, charity, and administration of the church.[27] During his tenure as archbishop of Salerno, Seripando carried out concretely the ideas expressed in Contarini's treatise.

Contarini's ideas were shared by many of the leading Catholic reformers of the day. Consequently, when Paul III formed a reform commission in 1536, under the leadership of Contarini, to draw up a report highlighting those areas in the Church most in need of reform, the commission reiterated many of the ideas expressed in the treatise. The commission's report, the *Consilium de emendanda ecclesia*, was presented to Paul III in 1537. In terms of the episcopacy, it highlighted the problem of non-residency, the root of all the other abuses that afflicted that office. The *Consilium* states that the bishop's duty of caring for his flock cannot be carried out in a satisfactory manner unless he is present among the people.

> The abuse that first and before all others must be reformed is that bishops above all and then parish priests must not be absent from their churches and parishes except for some grave reason, but must reside, especially bishops, as we have said, because they are the bridegrooms of the Church entrusted to their care.[28]

The *Consilium* not only made bishops aware of their duty to reside, but also paved the way for the great debates on this issue that would take place at the Council of Trent.

While many bishops neglected their duties, the example of some served as a reminder of the responsibilities of this office. Foremost among these was Gianmatteo Giberti, bishop of Verona (1524-1543), who embodied in his episcopacy the ideas expressed by Contarini and brought his experience to the reform commission that had drawn up the *Consilium*. As bishop of Verona, Giberti revived the pastoral mission of the bishop and the idea that the bishop must personally dedicate himself to the *cura animarum*. Giberti's efforts led to a thorough renewal and reform of his diocese that proved to be a model and inspiration for later bishops, including Seripando, who shared his understanding of the office.[29]

## SERIPANDO'S UNDERSTANDING OF THE EPISCOPAL OFFICE

Given the religious climate in the mid-sixteenth century, Seripando knew exactly what he needed to do to reform the diocese of Salerno. As soon as his nomination was confirmed by the pope, he set out to draw up a definite reform program that he could implement upon his arrival. The program that he drew up was that of the humanist reformers, associated with the ideas of such men as Gasparo Contarini and inspired by the example of Gianmatteo Giberti.

The first point in Seripando's reform program was the observance of episcopal residence, a sign of the bishop's seriousness about reform. He believed that a bishop first had to go to his diocese and give evidence that he did not consider his office merely the material basis for a dignified life of leisure or the springboard for higher ecclesiastical honors, but as a continuation of that office of teaching and ruling which Christ committed to the apostles.[30] In a letter written to the cathedral chapter shortly after his elevation to the episcopacy, Seripando emphasized the importance of residency: "As we are obligated, so we have determined to live, as long as we have left of this life, and to die among you and near the holy relics of the glorious apostle and evangelist Saint Matthew."[31]

As stated earlier, Seripando was unable to enter Salerno immediately upon his consecration. In a letter to his friend Augusto Cocciano in Rome, Seripando indicates that his expectation to enter Salerno quickly seemed "like a thousand years."[32] His desire to take possession of the diocese as quickly as possible must be understood in the context of his overall reform program, which rested on the idea of residence. For Seripando, residency was the foundation of a bishop's pastoral mission. He intended to present himself as a simple and humble pastor, a model of Christian conduct for both the clergy and the faithful. His preoccupation with the question of residency is seen in a letter he wrote to the governing council of Salerno: "Concerning Salerno I say to you, as I said to His Majesty, that as a result of my imperfection I can commit, and without a doubt I will commit, many errors in governing; but I will guard myself against one error — of never being absent by my own volition."[33] He expresses a similar sentiment to Cocciano: "I am able to commit — and due to my fragility I will commit — in this ministry many errors. But I will guard myself against one error as much as possible, namely, not to sin when it comes to residency, of which Your Excellency is able to recall what opinion I hold concerning this issue."[34] These were not empty words, since strict observance of residency characterizes Seripando's episcopacy. For six years he remained in his diocese without interruption. It was only in 1560, when the pope summoned him to Rome and subsequently in 1561 appointed him a legate to the Council of Trent, that Seripando was forced to absent himself from the personal governance of the diocese.

Since he was unable to assume his episcopal duties for several months after his consecration, in July 1554 Seripando named as his vicar general Domenico Capograsso, the archdeacon of the cathedral chapter. Seripando was not ignorant of the religious conditions among the clergy and the people in Salerno. He became more conscious of the situation the diocese found itself in as a result of the reports he received from his vicar. In addition, he utilized Capograsso to prepare the clergy and people of Salerno for the reform program he intended to implement upon his arrival.[35]

Besides his constant communication with his vicar general, Seripando received information on the state of Salerno from the cathedral chapter as well. A delegation from the chapter went to render homage to him in Naples in May 1554. During their visit with Seripando, members of the delegation acquainted him with the problems, especially financial, then confronting the chapter.[36]

Through these sources of information, Seripando came to Salerno well prepared and aware of the many problems he would have to confront. With the knowledge he possessed of the religious conditions of the clergy and the faithful, he began to develop a reform program that could be implemented in a preliminary way prior to his arrival in Salerno. In fact, on 29 June 1554, one month after the delegation from the cathedral chapter had visited him, they indicated that he had already begun to manifest himself as a true pastor of the church and of the clergy.[37]

When Girolamo Seripando took up residence in Salerno in September 1554, it was the first time in nearly a century that the clergy and the faithful had seen their bishop in their midst, proclaiming God's message to them and personally guiding them by word and example. The religious life of the people had declined and needed to be revitalized. Residence on the part of the bishop was seen by Seripando, as well as the Catholic reformers of the day, as the only means of accomplishing this goal.[38] Seripando, always aware of the problems of non-residency, used his elevation to the episcopacy to criticize his fellow bishops who continued to neglect this obligation. In his first sermon on the Lord's Prayer (1559), Seripando stated that in the Church of his day, the faithful were no longer in the hands of their pastors, but had been given over to mercenaries. He continued that bishops were more concerned with the accumulation of benefices and with temporal matters, than with the spiritual welfare of those entrusted to their care. Seripando exhorted his fellow bishops to restore the dignity of their office by undertaking the obligations of their office seriously.[39] The first step in this direction was residency.

Seripando did not need an external impetus to spur him on to his duties as archbishop. Numerous sketches that he had written in connection with the pastoral epistles of Saint Paul illustrate that he was intensively engaged with the primitive Church's ideal of the episcopate.[40] Seripando sought to realize in his episcopacy the Catholic Reformation's ideal of bishop as pastor and teacher according to the Pauline ideal. Based on 1 Timothy 3:2-7 and Titus 1:7-9, Seripando's sketches highlight those characteristics that he believed a bishop should possess. The bishop must be irreproachable, temperate, sober-minded, of good behavior, and hospitable. He must also be a good teacher, and in his teaching he must hold fast to the authentic message so that he will be able both to encourage the people to follow sound doctrine and to refute those who contradict it. Furthermore, the bishop should not be addicted to drink. He should be a man of gentleness and peace, not covetous, nor a lover of money. Moreover, he must manage his own house well and be well thought of by those outside the Church. Seripando concluded that since bishops are the custodians and pastors of souls, no one should seek this honor if he is not called to it by God.[41]

Seripando also expressed the need for a spiritual bond between the bishop and the faithful. The people of the diocese and the bishop should support one another through prayer; just as the bishop must pray for himself and for the people, so too must the people pray for themselves and for the bishop. Conscious of his fragility, the bishop has faith that the incessant prayer of his flock will assist him in being a good pastor.[42]

In addition to modelling his activity on the Pauline ideal of the bishop, Seripando also used the example of the great bishops of antiquity. He sought to restore the image of the bishop as found in the letters and sermons of the Church Fathers, in particular Ambrose, Augustine, Basil, and John Chrysostom, in which the bishop is both preacher and leader of his flock. Seripando highlights this in his first sermon on the Lord's Prayer: "Of these two things the Fathers and true pastors in the primitive Church took great care always to teach the people of the things pertaining to the faith and of the means to pray, because without faith no one can directly pray."[43] That this was no longer the case in Seripando's day is evident in a letter he wrote to Guglielmo Sirleto, saying it would please God if the bishops of his day would carry out their responsibilities and mirror the authority and dignity of the bishops of antiquity.[44] Given the current situation, Seripando called for prayers that this image would be restored once again.[45]

Shortly after his entrance into Salerno on 23 September 1554, Seripando began to expound upon his view of the office of bishop. One month after assuming office, he met with the clergy of his diocese, to whom he delivered a discourse entitled *De ingressu ad episcopatum*. He stated that the responsibilities of the office of bishop were never so burdensome in previous times as in their own because there had never been so much need for solicitude, vigilance, diligence, and care from those who exercised this ministry. Indeed, while the people of God are at the height of temptation, so that there is no vigilance that suffices, the holders of the episcopal office, according to Seripando, are not at the height of their duty. He indicates to the clergy that during the days of Augustine, as he himself attests, there was nothing more acceptable among men than the office of bishop, along with the office of priest or deacon. However, this was no longer true. Seripando complains, "Nothing is more odious than these offices today. Why? Jerome gives us the answer: 'Not all bishops are bishops!' The same can be said of the priests and deacons, because although in the place of the apostles we make use of their words, we do not imitate their behavior and austerity."[46]

As a result of this situation, the Church was in a state of decline. Furthermore, the people no longer looked upon the bishop, and clergy in general, as their leaders or the source of spiritual edification. In fact, Seripando observed that many among the laity considered themselves above the clergy. Consequently, he urged that bishops must see to it that they not only assume a position of leadership over their flock over whom they preside — with their sermons, their knowledge, and their conversation — but also priests, deacons, and all those in minor orders who were called to serve the Church of God.[47] Finally, he reminded the clergy that when Saint Paul writes in 1 Timothy 3:1 that whoever desires to be a bishop aspires to a noble task, he is signifying that the episcopacy is an office of service and not of honor, which it had become. Seripando recalls that the word "bishop," derived from the Greek, indicates that he is placed above those who have been entrusted to his care as an overseer. One cannot be considered a bishop, he contended, who merely desires to be superior over others and not work for the benefit of those entrusted to his care.[48] Thus, it is clear from this discourse with the clergy of Salerno that the bishop would devote his energy to the *cura animarum* and the religious formation of the people.

The instrument by which the religious formation of the people was to be accomplished was the sermon. Seripando considered preaching one of the most important duties of a bishop. As a successor to the apostles, he felt bound to announce the glad tidings of the gospel personally to his people. Seripando "considered it his first apostolic duty to preach the gospel by word and example, far more important than his pressing administrative duties. For him the sermon was an essential part of his duty as a spiritual shepherd."[49] Such a strong conviction on his part echoed the outlook of many rhetoricians and treatises on preaching in his day that "recalled that the Church Fathers were bishops whose 'particular duty' (*praecipuum munus*) was the ministry of the Word. . . . [Furthermore], in imitation of Christ who spent more time preaching than in every other ministry combined, the bishop continued the ministry."[50] Thus, soon after he took office Seripando began to preach to the people of Salerno. These sermons are important because they provide a glimpse into his understanding of the role and function of the bishop. The image of the bishop found in these sermons revives the patristic understanding of the bishop as teacher, pastor, and father.

Among the fundamental problems to which Seripando first directed his attention was the religious instruction of the faithful. He saw preaching as a means of providing this instruction, which he believed was lacking. Consequently, from the first day in Salerno as archbishop, Seripando revived the image of bishop as teacher. He believed that preaching was the principal obligation of the bishop, as he affirms in his first sermon on the Apostles' Creed: "Preaching the Word of God . . . is the first obligation placed on us by God, when he calls us to the ministry of the episcopacy: that we have to pasture his flock in the field of sacred scripture."[51]

In order for the bishop to be an effective teacher for his people, he must first read and meditate upon sacred scripture in order to learn from God and then teach the people what he has learned.[52] Seripando underlines how inseparable is the task of teaching from that of pastoring in the office of bishop. The bishop as teacher is not only one who teaches with wisdom, but also one who learns with patience. Seripando believes that it is necessary that bishops, besides teaching, must learn, because no one teaches better than he who each day grows and progresses, having learned better things.[53]

What should the focal point of the bishop's preaching be? First and foremost, the gospel. Unfortunately, as Seripando laments, this had been neglected by those who bore this responsibility, namely the bishops. As a result of this negligence, the gospel had not substantially penetrated the lives of the people.[54] Besides the gospel, bishops should teach the faithful the articles of faith, in particular those beliefs spelled out in the Creed; the Ten Commandments; the method of praying, especially the petitions of the Lord's Prayer; and the sacraments, emphasizing that they are means of grace.[55]

Throughout the history of the Church, but in particular at the time Seripando began his episcopal ministry, it was the primary task of the bishop, in his capacity as teacher, not only to communicate authentic doctrine according to tradition, but also to defend the Church's teaching against those who opposed it. Thus, the *defensio et tutela veritatis* was one of his principal duties. He enumerates several groups against whom the teachings of the faith needed to be guarded. Foremost among them are the sophists, who, in the frenzy to appear wise, fascinate and deceive with their words those who listen to them. Not less deceptive and hurtful, according to Seripando, are the hypocrites, who exploit the appearance of goodness to the damage of others; the traditionalists, who retain as true and just only what they are accustomed to hearing and doing through time; the artists, who aim only to please humanity and to flatter themselves; the rationalists, who, trusting only in their intelligence, not illuminated by faith, exclude themselves from access to authentic truth; lastly, those who do not hesitate to render false testimony consciously.[56]

Having singled out these groups, Seripando then illustrates how the bishop is to defend the truths of the faith against each one. He explains that the bishop safeguards the truth against the sophists by preaching and pointing out in every circumstance true wisdom; against the hypocrites by uncovering the wickedness of their actions; against the traditionalists by not hesitating to reject and to eliminate every shameful custom; against the artists by removing every abuse and permitting only what is in conformity with the Bible and the prescriptions of the Church; against the rationalists by uncovering, as Christ did, the blindness of their hearts; finally, against every false testimony by unmasking it without hesitation and with firmness.[57]

In fulfilling this task of both teacher and defender of the faith, Seripando was recalling bishops to the example of the bishops of antiquity. Those "diligent pastors and truly holy doctors," as Seripando refers to them in his first sermon on the Lord's Prayer, preached many sermons, wrote many treatises, and defended the faith against heretics, as they sought to pasture their flocks in the truths of the faith. For Seripando, it was time once again for bishops to teach and to preach to their people the divine doctrines of which they were the custodians.[58]

While the primary responsibility of the bishop was to instruct the faithful, the bishop was supposed to teach not only by word but also by deed. For Seripando, the preacher must first apply his knowledge to himself. Anyone who judges a preacher must not only see and hear him, but must also observe his deeds.[59] Basing his view on Paul's description of the episcopacy, Seripando believes that the bishop must reproach and combat the insubordinates, chatterboxes, and the deceivers not only with his words, but above all with the example of his good behavior. Herein lies the burden of the bishop, which is certainly more serious than the obligation of the ordinary Christian. If this burden is carried out well, it results in great glory, but if not, it invites a grave castigation.[60]

The importance which Seripando places on the demeanor of the bishop is evident in his eighth sermon on the Apostles' Creed (1556). In this sermon Seripando preaches that the duty of the true pastor is to lead others toward the truth by his example.[61] When the example of the bishop works against the truth, the consequences for the spiritual life of the faithful can be devastating. Seripando states:

> O my Lord, I beg you, out of your infinite mercy, when one of us evil pastors takes up the sword with our hands, and with our wicked deeds we offend your flock and we strike the ears of our people, that you will deign to heal the wounds we have inflicted, working within their souls, so that they will not despise the truth that we have preached to them. Lord, make them close their eyes to our wrongs and hateful operations, so that they will keep their ears sound and resolute to the good and true doctrine, and remain obedient to the just and honest commandments.[62]

Thus, the bishop who takes his responsibility to preach by word and example seriously restores the episcopal office to the task of the *cura animarum*. Seripando reiterates this again and again in his sermons as archbishop. In his first sermon on the Apostles' Creed, for example, Seripando states that Christ clearly indicated the principal responsibility of the bishop when he called Peter to head his Church, telling him that his office would be to feed his sheep and his lambs.[63] He expresses a similar idea in his first sermon on the Lord's Prayer, speaking of the primitive Church: ". . . the pastors had only one duty: to graze the flock of Jesus Christ in the Word of God."[64] As a result of their preaching, the bishops contributed to the flowering of the spiritual life of the Church and the faithful.[65] Because of the positive results of preaching, Seripando saw the bishop's task as one of expounding the Word of God, warning the faithful of their faults, and exhorting the people to live out the faith in their daily lives.[66]

Seripando desired to restore the office of bishop as pastor, whose primary duty was to preach the Word of God. Neglect of this duty opened the door to the ills of the Church. He, therefore, exhorted bishops to restore the dignity of their office: "This is my desire, which today it pleased God to have me discover, that we pastors return to our first and true office, to graze the sheep of Jesus Christ . . . and that we apply ourselves only to prayer and the ministry and interpretation of the Word of God."[67] The first duty, then, of those anointed in the Holy Spirit was to preach the gospel to the poor as Christ did. The principal aim of this preaching was to assist souls through theological teaching. For this reason he asked the faithful to pray for good preachers: "You should pray for, among so many other things, what I have told you, that God send preachers who purely and sincerely will preach the reign of God and who will be received by the people with respect, listened to with attention, and obeyed with works."[68]

By giving such prominence to preaching Seripando modelled himself on the bishops of ancient Christianity, who devoted themselves to the "spiritual ministry of the holy Word."[69] The bishops of the primitive Church delivered an abundance of sermons by which they nourished their flocks. It would be efficacious if bishops in his own day would follow their example by preaching and instructing the faithful. In this way, the bishop as successor of the apostles would not only be following the command of Christ to preach the gospel to all the world, but also assisting in the build-up of the Church by instructing the faithful in sound doctrine.[70]

Besides reviving the image of bishop as pastor and teacher, another characteristic of Seripando's episcopacy was his constant presence among his flock, with the care of a father, which led to the religious formation of his people. Like Augustine, Seripando considered the bishop a *paterfamilias*. From his noble position the bishop must, in whatever place and circumstance, defend Christ against every attack, respond to the murmurers or blasphemers and keep the faithful away from them, preserve them from heresy and correct not only those with whom he is familiar but everyone, on the condition, however, that he is moved only by love and he observes the norms of evangelical correction with the greatest prudence.[71] Just as the father of a family must provide the example for his household, so too the bishop, who must consider the faithful his children and members of his household. Seripando develops this notion in one of his sketches on the episcopacy:

> Whoever wants to have faithful children, who cannot be accused of extravagance and are respectful and obedient, let him [the bishop] be such. Whoever wants familiars who are temperate, modest, guided by upright habits, let the bishop be such. Whoever wants the others to be just, alien to strife and avarice, let him first refrain from such habits. If he does not want the others to engage in scandalous behavior, he should not behave in a way that gives rise to scandal and to this end, based on the example of Paul, he should refrain even from

those actions that are permissible for others, keeping in mind those who are weak in faith.[72]

That Seripando considered himself the father of his diocese is clear from his appointment as archbishop. Having been confirmed by the pope, he sent a letter of greetings to the cathedral chapter, in which he presented a synthesis of his pastoral reform program. He indicated in that letter that he was writing to the church and city of Salerno as their "father and pastor" (*"come Padre et Pastor vostro"*).[73] The sermons he preached as archbishop further support the image of bishop as father since, as he himself attests, the sermons grew out of a paternal affection for the people of Salerno.[74]

For Seripando, the responsibility of the bishop mirrors the responsibility of a father. Every father of a family carries, according to Seripando, the weight of examining, knowing, and acting on that which concerns his well-being and that of his own family, and to struggle against the ways of the world, the flesh, and the devil. The bishop is weighed down by the great burden to do all that for himself, his own family, and the entire diocese.[75] This burden, so full of responsibility that it allows him to announce with courage and credibility the word of God, and of a temperance which is truly exemplary, impresses upon him the effort of a like irreproachability.[76] Seripando refers to the bishop's duty to instruct the faithful as the "obligation of a father" (*"debito di padre"*).[77] In his first sermon on the Lord's Prayer, after reminding parents of their responsibility to teach their children the elements of the faith and prayer, Seripando observes: "And to me who am universal father of all, it is not enough that I know the tenets of the faith and the way to pray, but I must teach these things to all of you, who are my dear children."[78] Thus, as the father of a family has their needs always in his mind, so the bishop must direct all his thoughts to the salvation of the souls entrusted to his care.[79]

Seripando's understanding of the bishop as father meant that the responsibilities of the bishop extended beyond the ecclesiastical realm into the many concerns in the life of the city.[80] As mentioned previously, his nomination to the see of Salerno coincided with the period of political and economic crisis that resulted from the end of Ferrante Sanseverino's reign. Seripando, who truly saw himself as the father of the people, never hesitated to come to the city's aid, especially in the economic realm.

Whenever possible, he financially assisted the struggling educational institutions of the city, especially the university, and he also provided needed revenue for the government of the city. Thus, Seripando believed that the bishop as father should provide for both the spiritual and material needs of his flock.[81] In this way, the bishop, who generously watched over the people, truly provided a shepherd's care to his flock.

## Conclusion

Girolamo Seripando's understanding of the role and function of the bishop is a synthesis of the image of the bishop found in the Pauline epistles and in patristic practice. The bishop must undertake and exercise his office solely, Seripando contends, as a testimony of Christ's love. This love, which guides the bishop's ministry, is humble, unselfish, and generous. It is humble because it is conscious that the root of salvation is not found in being a bishop, but in being a Christian. This love is unselfish, because the flock must be grazed, not as one's own, but as belonging to Christ. It is generous because it is stronger than death.[82] Seripando writes:

> I do not equate the bishop to a captain of the army who, although he does not prepare everything with diligence and he does not do everything that is necessary for the safety and victory of his army, can save himself even if his army comes to be destroyed, but to a ship's steersman, who, guiding the ship in a sea tossed by strong winds, cannot save himself if with foresight he does not regulate everything for the protection of the ship and the crew.[83]

Appointed archbishop, Seripando sought to realize the image of bishop as pastor and teacher. In so doing, he implemented the notion of bishop as envisioned by the Catholic Reformation. The renewal of the episcopacy along these lines was at the forefront of discussions and debates prior to and during the Council of Trent. Seripando, whose efforts as archbishop of Salerno were inspired by this understanding and program, was one of the shining examples of episcopal renewal prior to the Tridentine legislation. As such, in Girolamo Seripando the bishop as preacher, teacher, and pastor of souls was once again at the heart of the Christian community.

## NOTES

1. Hubert Jedin, *Papal Legate at the Council of Trent, Cardinal Seripando*, trans. Frederic C. Eckhoff (St. Louis: B. Herder Book Co., 1947), 454.
2. David Gutiérrez, "Hieronymi Seripandi 'Diarium de Vita Sua' (1513-1562)," *Analecta Augustiniana* 26 (1963): 22, 82, 87.
3. BNN, MSS COD XIII, AA, vol. 61, f. 44.
4. BNN, Vind. Lat. 64, f. 17r.
5. Hubert Jedin and John Dolan, eds., *History of the Church* (New York: The Seabury Press, 1980), vol. 5, *Reformation and Counter Reformation*, by Erwin Iserloh, Joseph Glazik, and Hubert Jedin, 439.
6. Jedin, *Papal Legate*, 461.
7. H. Outram Evennett, *The Spirit of the Counter Reformation* (Cambridge: Cambridge University Press, 1968), 97. Also see John B. Tomaro, "San Carlo Borromeo and the Implementation of the Council of Trent," in *San Carlo Borromeo: Catholic Reform and Ecclesiastical Politics in the Second Half of the Sixteenth Century*, eds. John M. Headley and John B. Tomaro (Washington, DC: The Folger Shakespeare Library, 1988), 70-72.
8. Ibid., 97-98.
9. Hubert Jedin, *A History of the Council of Trent*, trans. Ernest Graf, vol. 2 (St. Louis: B. Herder Book Co., 1957), 334.
10. Jedin, *Papal Legate*, 658.
11. BAV, Vat. Lat. 6694, f. 304.
12. Jedin, *Papal Legate*, 396. The common obstacles to residency were the dispensation from the duty granted by the Curia; impeding of episcopal control through privileges of exemptions granted by the pope and on the part of secular rulers; and the frequent exclusion of bishops in the successive steps of judicial appeals. Despite these obstacles, Seripando had declared during the first period of Trent in the general congregation held on 21 June 1546 that "Absolutely no impediment exists that can excuse non-residence." He will hold on to this view throughout his life. For a discussion of the impediments to residency see Jedin, *A History of the Council of Trent*, 2:326-330.
13. Jedin, *Papal Legate*, 395.
14. Ibid.
15. Ibid.
16. Donato Dente, *Salerno nel Seicento: Nell'Interno di una città, vol. 2, pt. 1: Inediti per la storia Civile e Religiosa* (Salerno: Edisud, 1993), 290.
17. Rocchina M. Abbondanza, *Girolamo Seripando tra Evangelismo e Riforma Cattolica* (Naples: Ferraro, 1982), 26.
18. Dente, 290.

19. Alfredo Marranzini, "La figura del vescovo secondo Girolamo Seripando," in *Una Hostia: Studi in onore del Cardinale Corrado Ursi*, eds. Saturnino Muratore e Armando Rolla (Naples: M. D'Auria Editore, 1983), 211.
20. Jedin, *Papal Legate*, 470.
21. Gasparo Contarini, *De officio episcopi*, in *The Catholic Reformation: Savonarola to Ignatius Loyola*, ed. John C. Olin (Westminster, MD: Christian Classics, Inc., 1969), 91. Also see Elisabeth G. Gleason, *Gasparo Contarini: Venice, Rome, and Reform* (Berkeley: University of California Press, 1993), 93-98.
22. Ibid., 93.
23. Ibid., 95.
24. Ibid., 103.
25. Ibid., 104.
26. Ibid.
27. Marranzini, 212.
28. *Consilium de emendanda ecclesia*, in Olin, 191.
29. For a study of Giberti's episcopacy see Adriano Prosperi, *Tra evangelismo e controriforma: G.M. Giberti* (Rome: Edizioni di storia e letteratura, 1969).
30. Jedin, *Papal Legate*, 470-71.
31. Girolamo Seripando, "Lettere al capitolo," in Antonio Balducci, *Girolamo Seripando: Arcivescovo di Salerno, 1554-1563* (Cava dei Tirreni: Arti Grafiche di Mauro, 1963), 88.
32. Balducci, 14.
33. Generoso Crisci, *Il cammino della chiesa Salernitana nell'opera dei suoi vescovi*, 4 vols. (Naples: Libreria Editrice Redenzione, 1976-1984), 1: 532.
34. David Gutiérrez, "Españoles del siglo XVI en el epistolario de Seripando," *La Ciudad de Dios* 178 (1964): 246.
35. Balducci, 36-37.
36. Ibid., 14.
37. Ibid.
38. Jedin, *A History of the Council of Trent*, 2: 322.
39. Girolamo Seripando, "Prediche Salernitane," in Abbondanza, 88.
40. Jedin, *Papal Legate*, 471.
41. BNN, MSS COD VIII, AA, vol. 26, f. 40rv.
42. BNN, MSS COD VIII, AA, vol. 26, f. 31r.
43. PRS, 91.
44. BAV, Vat. Lat. 6189, f. 138.
45. "Lettera di Seripando a Camaiani," in Hubert Jedin, *Girolamo Seripando Sein Leben und Denken im Geisteskampf des 16 Jahrhunderts* (Wurzburg: Rita Verlag, 1937), 601-602.
46. BNN, MSS COD VIII, AA, vol. 26, f. 28v.
47. Ibid.

48. BNN, MSS COD VIII, AA, vol. 26, f. 24r-27r.
49. Jedin, *Papal Legate*, 471.
50. Frederick J. McGinness, *Right Thinking and Sacred Oratory in Counter-Reformation Rome* (Princeton: Princeton University Press, 1995), 17.
51. Francesco Linguiti, ed., *Prediche di Girolamo Seripando Arcivescovo di Salerno e poi Cardinale della S.R.C.* (Salerno: Raffaello Migliaccio, 1858), 41.
52. BNN, MSS COD VIII, AA, vol. 26, f. 27r.
53. BNN, MSS COD VIII, AA, vol. 26, f. 36v.
54. PS, 219-20.
55. BNN, MSS COD VIII, AA, vol. 26, f. 30v-31r.
56. BNN, MSS COD VIII, AA, vol. 26, f. 41v-44r.
57. Ibid.
58. PRS, 88.
59. Jedin, *Papal Legate*, 532-33.
60. Marranzini, 243.
61. PS, 147.
62. PS, 149.
63. PS, 41.
64. PRS, 87.
65. Ibid.
66. PS, 230.
67. PRS, 89.
68. PRS, 175.
69. PRS, 88.
70. PS, 219-20.
71. Marranzini, 234.
72. BNN, MSS COD VIII, AA, vol. 26, f. 30rv.
73. Balducci, 87.
74. PS, 42.
75. BNN, MSS COD VIII, vol. 26, f. 41r.
76. Marranzini, 242.
77. PRS, 92.
78. Ibid., 91.
79. BNN, MSS COD VIII, vol. 26, f. 27r.
80. BNN, MSS COD VIII, AA, vol. 26, f. 30r.
81. Balducci, 47.
82. BNN, MSS COD VIII, AA, vol. 26, f. 40v.
83. BNN, MSS COD VIII, AA, vol. 26, f. 38v.

CHAPTER FOUR

## THE SPIRITUAL TEACHINGS IN THE SERMONS OF GIROLAMO SERIPANDO

Since his early days in the Augustinian Order, Girolamo Seripando had been engaged in the ministry of preaching. He delivered sermons during the seasons of Advent and Lent in cathedrals and in the churches of the Augustinians to varied congregations ranging from the ordinary laity to princes and rulers. He also preached on great public occasions, as well as within the context of his visitations as prior general. It should not be surprising, then, that preaching came to hold a central place in the reform program he sought to implement as archbishop of Salerno.

While preaching remained a constant in Seripando's ecclesiastical career, the style and content of his sermons evolved over the years. In the judgment of his contemporaries, during the 1520s and 1530s he derived the principal subjects of his sermons from Platonic theology. "The contemplative preoccupation with the world of nature and of the mind, the steps that lead up to divine beauty, the study of 'divine wisdom,' were the interests of his life and thinking, and therefore they formed the contents of his sermons."[1] The choice of such themes resulted from Seripando's own intellectual interests, as well as reflecting the humanist background of those to whom these sermons were addressed. While such learned sermons won the admiration of the members of the Neapolitan humanist circles, they were not popular among the ordinary population. Despite the fact that these sermons were addressed to the intellect rather than the heart, Seripando's cultural preparation and intellectual ability made him a sought-after preacher in the principal cities of Italy.[2]

Since the content of his sermons reflected his interest in humanist Platonism, homilies on the scriptures, the ecclesiastical year, and the liturgy were not in the forefront during this phase of his preaching activity. Whenever Seripando did employ passages from scripture he did so only as dogmatic proofs or as the basis for systematic reasoning.[3] The main object of these Platonic sermons was to build a bridge between the tenets of Platonic theology and the needs of human living. After the 1530s, Seripando began to shift his attitude, believing that scripture was to be used for more than speculative treatment or the accumulation of literary parallels. He realized that the sermon was meant to open up an understanding of God's word and explain the religious and moral life.[4] This understanding will characterize the sermons he delivered as archbishop of Salerno.

## SERIPANDO'S SERMONS AS ARCHBISHOP OF SALERNO

Upon his arrival in Salerno, Girolamo Seripando placed a great deal of importance on the religious instruction of the faithful. One of the most effective means of transmitting religious teaching and doctrine was preaching. Consequently, from his first day in Salerno as archbishop, Seripando remained faithful to this task, which he considered his principal obligation as a bishop. As we have seen, as a successor to the apostles, he felt bound to announce the good news of the gospel to the faithful personally.

Seripando preached to the people of Salerno regularly throughout the ecclesiastical year, as well as on special occasions. Between 1554-1560 he preached sermons that revolved around particular themes and formed a homiletic cycle. The first set of sermons, between 1554-1555, utilized the Pauline letters and revolved around the theme "on the manner of receiving Christ." Between 1555-1556 Seripando's sermons commented on Psalm 48; an exposition of the Apostles' Creed served as the basis of the sermons given between 1556-1557; and a commentary of the Lord's Prayer, along with an explanation of sacramental doctrine, formed the content of his sermons between 1559-1560.[5] In addition to these sermons, Seripando records in his diary the preaching of forty-seven sermons during this six-year period on such special occasions as the feast commemorating the dedication of the cathedral and the two feasts in honor of Saint Matthew, whose relics were venerated in the cathedral.[6] These sermons, whose main purpose was not to admonish but to build up the Christian way of life in the listeners, reveal Seripando's awareness of the deficiencies present in the religious, spiritual, and social life of his flock. The sermons aim at addressing the specific problems of the laity by providing them with sound Christian teaching, counsel, and practical suggestions which would allow for a personal regeneration and renewal, leading toward the living out of the Christian life.[7] In short, Seripando hoped that his sermons would teach the faithful how to live according to their religion by allowing Christianity to permeate their daily lives.[8]

In this way Seripando anticipates the Tridentine legislation that not only required the bishops to preach, but also gave preaching a central role in the bishop's pastoral mission. As one who had actively engaged in preaching prior to his elevation to the episcopacy, he knew how efficacious preaching was in the attempt to overcome the growing difficulties that the Church encountered in regulating the moral life of society, which had greatly declined, as well as criticizing the superficial and superstitious elements within Christianity.[9]

As one who prefigures and faithfully interprets the Tridentine decrees on preaching, Seripando aims to assist souls through the preaching of sermons. While the object of his sermons remained theology, it was a theology applied to the pastoral needs of the faithful. This involved meditating on the Scriptural text and applying the message of scripture to the situation in which the people found themselves. Seripando employed the sermon not only as a means to preach on such themes as sin, forgiveness, and justification, but also, and perhaps more importantly, to provide the faithful with religious instruction that was simple, accessible, and responsive to their spiritual needs.[10] Thus, he often employed a simple cathechetical approach.

Seripando's approach reflected the common view that the pulpit was the place from which the teachings of the Church could most easily be transmitted to the people. He saw the sermon as the most suitable means to elevate the religious, moral, and cultural level of the diverse social groups within the population who were, for the most part, illiterate.[11] Seripando reduced theological ideas and problems to practical concerns, to the realities in the lives of his listeners. He aimed not only to teach doctrine in his sermons, but also to correct the customs and habits of the people to move them toward a spirit of inner renewal.

## PREACHING STYLES IN THE SIXTEENTH CENTURY

The preaching style utilized by Seripando as archbishop of Salerno reflects the changes that were taking place in sixteenth century preaching. The revival of interest in classical antiquity during the Renaissance had an important effect on the style of preaching and the content of sermons. The preaching manuals that surfaced both prior to and after Trent, while not intended to suppress the medieval form of preaching, reflect the widespread and growing practice in Italy, and Europe in general, of applying the principles of classical oratory to preaching the Word.[12] Thematic in structure, the medieval scholastic sermon, with its focus on abstract doctrine, had as its principal aim *docere*.[13] During the Renaissance preachers began to adapt and use the classical rhetorical form, thereby broadening the scope and content of the sermon. Not only was the sermon meant to teach doctrine to the listeners, but also to move them to action through persuasion.[14] This entailed moving the whole person, mind, heart, and soul. "Persuasion meant teaching the faithful, moving them to act in accordance with their faith, and having them delight in hearing the word preached. . . . Preachers felt less given to theological speculation and teaching than to describing vividly . . . the greatness of the divine mysteries, the majesty of God, or the wisdom of the faith."[15] The success of persuasion was measured by the extent to which an individual was moved to a better way of life.[16]

Among those responsible for this shift in emphasis was Erasmus, whose work on sacred oratory, the *Ecclesiastes*, was published in 1535. In this work Erasmus defines preaching as an act of teaching, but a different type of teaching from that found in the medieval sermon. "For Erasmus, truly Christian teaching is never dialectical or argumentative, never frigidly abstract, for it must always be persuasive of a godly life."[17] Consequently, Erasmus located the sermon in the genre of deliberative oratory, giving it a greater moralistic quality since it was most often addressed to a group of ordinary people.[18]

Given the moral tone of the sermon, by the middle of the sixteenth century the gospel came to be linked in "preaching theory with a turning from vice and an embracing of virtue, under threat of punishment and the hope of reward."[19] Preachers began to paint a picture of a religion based on sin and atonement, where salvation was possible to those willing to alter their way of life.[20] Since the preacher taught ordinary people, among whom many were illiterate, he would develop his theological or doctrinal theme using familiar, simple language, so that people could understand, often employing images from family life and human relations. Concerned with teaching people the way to salvation, "the central theme of late medieval Catholic theology was that God gave man the ability to cooperate with grace, to do what was in him. The preachers did not demand the impossible, but insisted that man's creation in God's image allowed him to participate in the business of his own salvation."[21] As a result, preachers were more concerned with moral reformation and inner renewal than condemnation.

This emphasis gave rise to a series of treatises on preaching that contributed to a new understanding of the sermon. In 1543 Alfonso Zorilla published *De sacris concionibus recte formandis*, the first treatise on preaching printed in Italy that broke with the medieval style. Zorilla saw the sermon as an informal, familiar discourse between the preacher and the congregation.[22] In 1555 Christopher of Padua, Seripando's successor as prior general of the Augustinian Order, issued directives for preachers within the Order. Christopher indicated that the style of preaching must be simple and sincere, since its aim is to persuade people to live according to the spirit and not according to the flesh.[23] To accomplish this, the preacher should emphasize merely those things that will further build up the faith.[24] Thus, the preacher should follow the safe doctrine of the Church and the Fathers, being careful not to stray from this. The directives offer a simple method of preaching to ensure this. First, the preacher should propound the true and Catholic beliefs of the faith, then he should diligently expound on these beliefs, and finally, he should confirm these beliefs with scripture, tradition, conciliar documents, and the writings of the Church Fathers.[25] These directives, which Seripando reflected in his sermons as archbishop, were meant to encourage the preaching of sermons that would touch the hearts of people and persuade them to live out their faith.

After Seripando's death, later treatises continued to alter the preaching style of the period. In 1576 Diego de Estella published his *Modus concionandi*, which turned the teaching of the sermon to a moral purpose. According to de Estella, the preacher should focus on the moral sense of scripture, aiming to move the audience away from sin to a life of virtue and good works.[26] Luis de Granada, following Erasmus' idea about preaching, viewed the sermon as persuading individuals to live a life of justice and piety.[27]

This moralistic quality and persuasive character was clearly evident in the sermons Seripando preached during his tenure as archbishop of Salerno. While he was not unique in preaching such sermons, they differed in character and in tone from many of the penitential sermons preached throughout Italy during the Renaissance. Concerned with reconciling the individual with God, the penitential sermons often exhorted the faithful to practice mortifications that would foster a spirit of repentance.[28] Seripando, however, was more concerned with moral reformation and inner renewal. As a result, he embodied a more Erasmian attitude toward preaching, avoiding elaborate theological discussions or rhetorical discourses. Seripando desired to move his listeners to cultivate their religious and spiritual life by presenting them with simple explanations of the elements of the faith.

In this way, Seripando anticipated the Tridentine legislation requiring bishops to preach to their people. During its fifth session, the Council of Trent decreed that the preaching of the gospel was the chief task of the bishop. The Council also stipulated that preaching was to be adapted to the mental capacities of the people. It was clear too about the content of sermons, indicating that those charged with the office of preaching were

> to feed the people committed to them . . . by teaching them those things that are necessary for all to know in order to be saved, and by impressing upon them with briefness and plainness of speech the vices that they must avoid and the virtues that they must cultivate, in order that they may escape eternal punishment and obtain the glory of heaven.[29]

As a faithful interpreter of this decree, Seripando during his tenure as archbishop of Salerno worked to restore the teachings and the spirit of the gospel in the lives of the people of the diocese.

## THE CATECHETICAL SERMONS

The preaching manuals of the day instruct preachers to develop the sermon to meet the needs of the congregation. Since the congregation was often composed of several different social classes, preachers commonly refer to the different orders of society that were present.[30] It is clear from Seripando's sermons that he followed such directives. His sermons reveal his acute awareness of the defects that existed in the religious and spiritual life of his flock. He addressed in great detail the specific problems facing the laity, cognizant that only continuous and suitable preaching, accompanied by sound Christian teaching, counsel, and practical directives, rather than threats of punishment, would encourage a personal regeneration and renewal that would lead toward the living out of the Christian life.[31] Preaching in Italian, Seripando employed lively imagery related to the lives of the people of Salerno to provide them with indispensable principles to purify and vivify their faith.

As bishop, Seripando was above all an interpreter of scripture. Like his great model Augustine, he did not tie himself to the literal meaning of the text but strove to understand each individual passage within the context of the whole Bible. In contrast to the addresses he gave as prior general of the Augustinians, Seripando's sermons as bishop were geared far more to fundamental catechesis, explaining the liturgy, the sacraments, the basic truths of the faith, and prayer. Increasingly, he preached catechetical sermons as he became conscious of the religious needs of the congregation and of his duty to provide them with the means to purify and animate their faith. The most noteworthy of his catechetical sermons were the cycle on the Apostles' Creed and the cycle on the Lord's Prayer. In these sermons, "the explanations avoided all rhetorical affectation and were based on a profound knowledge of scripture and the writings of the Fathers, but throughout they breathed the spirit of the preacher's personal piety and thus satisfied the religious needs of his hearers."[32] Additionally, in these sermons Seripando provided his listeners with practical directives to assist them in the living out of their spiritual and religious lives. In doing so, he did not spare them from any unpleasant truth.

Seripando refers to the sermons on the Creed and the Lord's Prayer as "intimate reflections" (*"famigliari ragionamenti"*) between the shepherd and his flock.[33] More revealing than the sermons on the Creed are those on the Lord's Prayer, which

Seripando characterizes as "conversations" and "entertainments" ("*intertenimenti*") with the faithful standing around their bishop to have the faith explained to them.[34] These sermons are more personal than those on the Creed. Not only are they filled with illustrations and examples from the current situation in Salerno, but Seripando often interrupts his thoughts to lament what he perceives as problems or to provide practical directives. He knew how to captivate with his stories all those present in the congregation, from children to adults, and to mingle strictness with kindness.

The catechetical sermons reflect Seripando's belief that preaching formed an essential part of the bishop's pastoral obligations. His aim was to teach the faithful with the words of Jesus himself. To realize this aim, he adapted the content and message of the sermon to the capacity of the hearers. He employed the sermon as part of his vast program to teach the people not only the doctrines of the faith, but also the means to pray, which in turn stirs up the faith in the individual's heart.[35] Thus, he warned the faithful against the mechanical rattling off of the Lord's Prayer. He urged them to pray the words slowly and reverently, seeing in its petitions not a burden on the faithful, but those precepts that teach individuals how to live Christian lives.[36] Seripando spells this out in his second sermon on the Lord's Prayer:

> When you say, "Hallowed be thy name," do you not realize that God desires and commands that his name be sanctified by all? When you say, "Thy kingdom come," do you not comprehend that God wants and commands that his kingdom be desired and waited for by everyone? When you say, "Thy will be done," who does not know that it is pleasing to God that his faithful do not concern themselves with their own will, but remain always content that in all things they do God's will? When you say, "Our daily bread," who is so blind that he does not see that every good thing both temporal and spiritual, because both are necessary in life, must be recognized each day as coming from the hand of God? . . . When you say, "And forgive us our trespasses," is there any person in the world so stupid that he does not understand the gospel precept to forgive one's enemies? Without observing this command one cannot obtain nor hope for the remission of sins from God. And when you say, "And lead us not into temptation," do you not see that it is commanded that in the battle of this life you vigorously struggle, trusting however more in God's help than in yourselves?[37]

Thus, by applying the message of scripture to the religious and moral life, Seripando hoped that his sermons would assist souls in the living out of the spiritual life in the midst of their daily activities and concerns.

## SPIRITUAL THEMES IN SERIPANDO'S SERMONS

### CHARITY

The economic and social conditions present in Salerno often influenced the content of Seripando's sermons. Of major concern was the gap between the rich and the poor, and the responsibility the former had toward the latter. This was a common theme among preachers throughout early modern Europe. Because of their defense of the rights of the needy, preachers often came under heavy criticism from the wealthier members of society. The focus on society's lack of charity was not an uncommon theme in medieval or early modern preaching. Still, the fact that it had dominated the sermons of the sixteenth century suggests that this problem may have become more pronounced at this time.[38] Despite the fact that Seripando also delivered sermons on this theme, he emphasized the need for charity as a means of fostering a penitential spirit among the members of his congregation. Furthermore, as a humanist, Seripando believed that charity was the basis for a spirituality which translated to activity in the world. This active spirituality was also widespread in Italy during the sixteenth century.[39]

As a member of the Augustinians, Seripando strongly emphasized the notion of charity, which is the fundamental principle of Augustinian spirituality. Saint Augustine demonstrated that charity is the vital point of Christianity. To it he reduces the scriptures, to it he inspires exegesis, in it he brings together the content of theology, morality, pedagogy, catechetics, the life and justice of Christianity.[40] Saint Augustine developed a theology of charity as the essence of Christian perfection, the soul of the Church, and a gift of God. Charity, as the fundamental principle in his spirituality, allows an understanding of the relations of the soul with God and allows an organization of doctrine and the means of sanctification, which gives direction to the life of the spirit.[41] Thus, charity is the source and soul of the spiritual life, since it generates within the soul a desire for and movement toward God. Saint Augustine places charity at the center of his spiritual conception. The triumph of charity is fulfilled through the discovery of the current of love that moves our being toward the Eternal One, through the opinion of the impotence of this love to attain naturally the goal to which it aspires, through the participation in the common good.[42]

For Seripando, charity is the basis for a renewal of the Christian life. In his third sermon on the Lord's Prayer, Seripando indicates that in this prayer the believer seeks from God not only faith and hope, but also charity, which leads to perfection. This perfection is attained by incorporating within one's life the two precepts of charity. The first is to love God like a father, which means to love him with all one's heart, mind, and soul. The second is to love one's neighbor like a brother or sister.[43] Seripando explains: "Saint Paul says in one of his letters that charity is the perfection of the law, and, in another letter having demonstrated this, states that all the law is fulfilled in the precept: Love your neighbor as yourself (Romans 13:8-10)."[44] This second precept calls for a life of action that flows out of contemplation. Seripando asks,

> How can the Christian who dedicates himself to contemplation not leave this state immediately in order to give himself to action whenever his neighbor needs his service of love? . . . Who, likewise, would be so dedicated to action not to be in need every so often of contemplation? Or at least when he prays, does not elevate his mind to God from all his earthly cares?[45]

Thus, because of the importance of charity toward one's neighbor in Seripando's thought, the Christian life is neither one of contemplation nor of action alone, but a fusion of the two as the individual attempts to fulfill the command of Christ to love God and neighbor.

In his fourteenth sermon on the Lord's Prayer, Seripando directs the congregation's attention to the practical implications of Christ's precept to love one another. He exhorts the faithful not to forget the seven corporal works of mercy which must be carried out in the Church until the end of time, and reminds them that in assisting one's neighbor one is actually assisting Jesus. Paraphrasing the famous judgment scene in the gospel of Matthew (Matthew 25:31-46), Seripando states:

> Christ himself says that when one who is hungry is fed, he is fed; when one who is thirsty is given to drink, he is given to

drink; when a pilgrim is received, he is received; when one who is naked is clothed, he is clothed; when one who is ill is visited, he is visited; when one who is imprisoned is consoled, he is consoled. . . . Christ views these works as if they were done to him.[46]

Thus, one cannot say that one loves Christ without loving those most in need. Seripando's point is clear. By incorporating charity within one's life one can be transformed into a spiritual being. This occurs because one moved by charity is open to God's will and presence, allowing for a transformation of the self.[47] Therefore, Seripando exhorted the people of Salerno to surrender their wills to the will of God if they wish to be renewed and transformed into spiritual beings.[48]

While acts of charity could assist one in the movement toward perfection, Seripando also recognized that the desire to perform such acts would result only from a life which had begun to experience inner renewal. A main concern for Seripando, this was the object of his sermons. In his first sermon on the Apostles' Creed Seripando explained to the faithful that it was his desire to implant Christ into their hearts so that the Word of God would bear fruit in their lives and actions.[49]

The need for inner renewal and its link with good works toward others is also highlighted in Seripando's treatment of the petition "hallowed be thy name" ("*sanctificetur nomen tuum*"). In the sixth sermon on the Lord's Prayer, he reminds the faithful to preserve themselves in justice and to walk along the paths of justice, namely avoiding evil and doing good. Seripando states: "These are the ways that lead us to that blessed city . . . where . . . nothing stained can enter, nor anything which can dominate, nor lies, because in that city reigns true purity. . . ."[50] Those who lead good lives will be sanctified and brought into the company of the angels to glorify, praise, and bless God's holy name.[51]

## SACRED SCRIPTURE

One's desire to perform works of charity would result from a knowledge of sacred scripture. Once again it is evident that Seripando's ideas emerge from the Augustinian spiritual tradition, which is evangelical in nature. For Augustine, the Bible was not only the basis for religious instruction, but also the fount of spiritual formation. He considered the Bible the expression of God's will and intelligence. The truths found in the

Word of God lead one toward a spiritual joy.[52] It is a pure joy that results from the purification of evil, since one abandons oneself to true piety and union with God. Through the reading of scripture one is humbled and is thrust toward the praise of God.

As previously stated, for Seripando the sermon was intended to open up an understanding of God's Word and indicate an application to the religious and moral life. This in turn would lead to an inner renewal of the individual and assist the individual in the living out of the spiritual life. This call to inner renewal appears most clearly in his treatment of the petition "give us this day our daily bread" (*"panem nostrum quotidianum da nobis hodie"*). Seripando focuses on the significance of the word *"panem."* Among its many meanings, *"panem"* refers to the Word of God. For the humanists of the day, the study and understanding of scripture would lead to an inner renewal and regeneration, thereby revivifying one's religious life. The humanist program of a return *ad fontes* provides elements not found in earlier reflections on the theme of scripture as food for the soul.[53] Seripando embodies this view when he states that God gave to humanity the bread which gives life to the soul, namely his Word.[54] He writes: "The gospel is, thus, the bread of life, of intellect, bread in which man truly lives . . . bread which is needed every day."[55] This bread, which is the word and commandment of God, is eaten when one obeys what God says and commands. Thus, in the Word of God humanity lives.[56] For this reason, Seripando concludes, it is necessary either to hear or to read the Word of God daily, because this bread is needed to sustain one's spiritual life in the same way in which bread is needed to sustain one's physical life.[57] Given this outlook, the bishop suggests to his listeners that at the end of each day they ask themselves whether or not they have heard or read the Word of God.[58]

Because of the importance of scripture in the cultivation of the spiritual life, Seripando reminds the faithful that scripture is the source of certain and infallible truth. Consequently, every Catholic is compelled to adhere firmly to what scripture teaches, even to those ideas in scripture which seem contrary to our natural discourse or to the sayings of the wise of this world. For this reason, Seripando points out, Saint Paul says that the faithful Christian must subjugate his intellect to Jesus Christ, because in doing so he cannot deviate from the wisdom of the Father, which is the truth, the way, and the life.[59] By incorporating the truths found in scripture into one's life, the individual would experience the inner renewal of his religious life. Seripando made this clear in his twelfth sermon on the Lord's Prayer:

> In saying *"panem"* our minds run to the bread of true life, to the word of God, eternal food, the Word for our salvation. As expressed in the holy letters, the word for our salvation was incarnated and for this reason we say *"nostrum."* Without this bread given to us, our soul dies a far worse death than that of our body. Since we desire the true life, for this reason we confess that we have need of this bread every day saying *"quotidianum."* And thus, every day we seek this bread saying, *"da nobis,"* as it pleased you, Lord, to give it to our holy Fathers, who by this bread lived, by this bread were made strong, by this bread were consoled, by this bread were renewed. With this bread they walked toward heaven.[60]

Seripando believed that his listeners would experience the same effects and would realize the same spiritual benefits through the daily reading or hearing of the scriptures.

## LAY PIETY

Girolamo Seripando's emphasis on scripture as a means to the cultivation of the spiritual life reflects one of the basic characteristics of humanist spirituality, namely a piety which is biblically based. Gaining inspiration from the Scriptural text, the humanists emphasized a piety that gave no advantage to the religious, but rather recognized gradations of spirituality in which the laity could hope to attain the highest level of perfection. Within humanist circles there developed a growing sense of the "dignity of the lay estate" and the need to portray Christian piety in lay terms.[61] Such a view acknowledged that all Christians, not merely the religious, shared in common the goal of striving for perfection.

This outlook was also at the heart of many of the confraternities that were founded in Italy during the late medieval and early modern periods. Realizing that the laity lived in different circumstances than the clergy, the statutes of many confraternities prescribed a manner of religious life for laymen that insisted on the social virtues of charity and humility. The statutes of many confraternities enjoined upon their members the practical elaboration of a moral theology of prayer, penitence, and good works.[62]

In developing a lay person's approach to spiritual matters the humanists focused on prayer, especially the Lord's Prayer. In calling for adherence to biblical models of prayer, in particular the petitions of the Lord's Prayer, Erasmus was instrumental in developing this approach. Erasmus justifies this emphasis not only because it is the "only prayer that Jesus taught to his disciples" but also because the Church Fathers believed that "nothing at all should be sought of God beyond those things which the Lord prescribed for us in the Lord's Prayer."[63] The life of prayer for Erasmus was one of progress and stages in which the religious and clerical order had no advantage over the laity.

Seripando also shared this aspect of humanist spirituality. He did not distinguish the religious from the laity in their efforts to strive for spiritual perfection. While the former strove for perfection through the living out of the evangelical counsels, he believed that all Christians, regardless of their station in life, were called to imitate Christ and to move toward perfection through charity, which reflects the fullness of the gospel.[64]

In the sermons on the Lord's Prayer, Seripando makes clear that there are no first-class or second-class Christians. Rather, there is only one following of Christ to which all are obligated. This view is apparent in the seventh sermon on the Lord's Prayer, which revolves around Matthew 16:24, where Jesus said to his disciples: "If anyone wishes to come after me, let him deny himself, and take up his cross, and follow me." Seripando states that the religious interpret this passage not as a commandment to all Christians, without which one cannot be saved, but rather as evidence that one who embraces the evangelical counsels will achieve spiritual perfection more easily and more quickly.[65] He continues by pointing out that the religious believe that through their vows of poverty, chastity, and obedience they have denied their very selves. While one should praise those who have attained perfection through the living out of these evangelical counsels, Seripando reflects upon the laity and their obligation to strive for perfection: "I cry out in a loud voice to whoever will listen: this teaching is not merely a counsel given to [the religious], but is a precept given to you, because you too are called to be good disciples of Christ. For this reason you must also deny yourselves."[66] Seripando explains that the laity are not called to deny themselves through the living out of the evangelical counsels, but rather by not placing confidence in their own strength, in their own minds, in short, by abandoning themselves to Christ and placing their lives and hope in him. In this way they will achieve that same perfection associated with the living out of the evangelical counsels and attain the salvation promised to all who follow Christ.[67]

The laity would arrive at this understanding of perfection through prayer, the focal point of this lay-oriented humanist spirituality. Seripando reflects this concern for a spirituality of prayer that would reach a lay audience in his first sermon on the Lord's Prayer. He relates a story to his congregation in which a young man asks his bishop for a small book on the Christian life which he can always carry with him. The bishop hands the young man the Creed and the Lord's Prayer. Seripando explains:

> What could be written or read that would be more brief? What could be put to memory more easily? The prophet said: whoever shall invoke the name of the Lord will be saved. For this you need the Lord's Prayer. Saint Paul said: How is it possible for him who has no belief to invoke God? For this you need the Creed. In these two prayers are found all that is needed for the inner worship of God, which consists of faith, hope, and love. The obligation of faith is to believe. The obligation of hope is to pray. The obligation of charity is to love.[68]

Thus, through prayer the laity can achieve the same goal of perfect love which results from the living out of the evangelical counsels.

### PENANCE

While prayer was an essential element of the laity's progress toward perfection, Seripando also emphasized the recognition of one's failures and shortcomings through the reading of scripture which would spur one to a *metanoia*. Given this, he offered another meaning for the word *"panem"* in his sermons on the Lord's Prayer, namely, the "bread of tears," since when the pain of one's sinfulness is strong and touches the heart, it gives rise to tears.[69] He indicated that this bread is eaten when one is truly sorry for one's sins: "It cannot be denied that [this bread] will not be hard and bitter, but it is softened and sweetened with the memory that other penitents who ate this bread obtained the remission of their serious sins and enormous wickedness."[70] Seripando indicated that true repentance takes place when one realizes the pain of having offended God, of having been ungrateful to God, of having broken the commandments of God.[71]

In order for the process of repentance to take place, one must acknowledge one's sinfulness. Seripando exhorts the faithful each day to acknowledge that in some way they have sinned:

> My dear children, say, today I have committed some sin; today I want to be sorry. I want to repent, I want to implore mercy and grace. "Da nobis," this word makes us aware that true repentance is a gift from God, who grants it to those he wishes. . . . But we, aware of our infirmity, ask for forgiveness from God saying *"da nobis hodie."* And why today? Because you do not know if there will be time to receive forgiveness tomorrow.[72]

For Seripando, then, the word *"panem"* in the Lord's Prayer is a reminder of God's promise to the sinner that he who repents, he who eats this bread of sorrow, will not only be forgiven, but will also be blessed by God with the fullness of his grace.[73] Here the bishop is not merely calling upon the faithful to acknowledge their sinfulness, but he is also pointing to the need to receive the sacrament of penance. His concern was twofold. In the first place, Seripando defends the power of the Church to forgive sins against those who attacked this notion. In the fourteenth sermon on the Apostles' Creed he makes it clear that there was no remission of sins outside the Church. This power to bind and loose was given to Peter by Christ, and therefore, Seripando stresses, whoever believes that this power is found in the Church and turns away from sin will receive remission of his sins. On the other hand, those who do not believe that this power is found in the Church will not receive remission of their sins and will fall into a state of hopelessness. Seripando makes it clear that from the days of the apostles, penance and the remission of sins within the Church have been preached.[74]

Seripando's second concern was that the faithful postponed going to confession, thereby jeopardizing their eternal salvation. In the ninth sermon on the Apostles' Creed, he explicitly raises the issue:

> When do you want to confess yourselves? The women will say, "Christmas Eve." And how do you know that you will be able to that day? Wouldn't tomorrow be better? Wouldn't today be better? The men will respond, "It is enough to confess during Holy Week." And how can you be sure that you will arrive at

Holy Week, since you cannot be certain of even one hour of life? Who will be able to be assured that at that moment of death the matters of the soul can be attended to? Do not put your faith in such time.[75]

Seripando's emphasis on the sacrament of penance did not stem merely from a concern to fulfill a canonical requirement. Rather, it is clear that the act of confession assisted the individual in the cultivation of a penitential spirit that would lead to the conversion of the sinner. The sense of sorrow that one felt for one's sins not only moved one toward confession, but also initiated this process of conversion within the individual's heart. According to Seripando, the heart of a sinner is like a stone that needs to be softened and broken by a true spirit of contrition.[76] This spirit of contrition results not from a fear of God's punishment, but rather out of a love of God that has been offended by sin. One's need for confession stems from the recognition of one's sinfulness that surfaces from a spirit of contrition. For Seripando, the contrite of heart are healed and restored by God.[77] The bishop's emphasis on confession stems from a positive view of the effect of this sacrament on the individual, namely, the renewal and regeneration of one's life.

Among the many questions raised during the sixteenth century concerning sin and its forgiveness was the certainty that one's sins had been remitted. Seripando explores this issue in the seventeenth sermon on the Lord's Prayer, in which he outlines certain "signs" that the individual should look for that can assure him of having been granted a remission of sins. The first sign, according to Seripando, is faith, which, as is read in the scriptures, the Lord sent to the sinners indicating that it was their faith that saved them.[78] The second sign is charity, of which the Lord said, when he forgave the sins of Mary Magdalene, that her many sins had been forgiven because she had shown charity toward others. Conversion is the third sign because, according to Seripando, this involves a change in the soul from evil thoughts, desires, and works to good thoughts, desires, and works. The repentance of the sinner is a further sign of the remission of sins. One who is truly penitent walks according to the commandments of life and will not die but live eternally. A strong sign that one's sins have been forgiven is the tears of the sinner. Seripando indicates that tears are so powerful that they cause God to forget one's sins and erase them as if they had never been committed. Finally, he states that when one recites the words of the Lord's Prayer "forgive us our trespasses" ("*dimittimus debitoribus nostris*") and feels in the depths of one's soul a true sense of forgiveness, this is a true and clear sign that the Father in heaven has pardoned those sins that have offended him.[79] The presence of each of these signs in the life of the penitent sinner allows the individual to progress toward a genuine reform of one's life, which results from a true spirit of repentance.

Given the importance of repentance, Seripando reminds parents of their responsibility to teach their children about the need to be penitent. He likens the need to be repentant to that of physical cleanliness. In his sixth sermon on the Lord's Prayer he states:

> Listen, fathers, listen, mothers. You are diligent in keeping your children clean. You wash their heads often. When their faces, hands, or articles of clothing are dirty, you correct them and say to them that it is bad manners to dirty oneself and not wash oneself immediately or to be seen with dirt stains on one's clothing and shoes. Why don't you also say to them, "My children, by the grace of God you are washed from sin in baptism. Keep yourselves clean and pure by no longer sinning. If you do sin, immediately cleanse yourselves through penance."[80]

While the repentant sinner can experience forgiveness, Seripando also makes it clear that the individual should avoid falling into sin in the midst of temptation. In his nineteenth sermon on the Lord's Prayer, he reminds his listeners that because life is full of temptations, they would be exposed to sin and possibly fall into sin once again. This battle against sin and temptation begins from the moment of baptism and is present every day of one's life until the moment of death.[81] Thus, people must arm themselves so as to be able to help and defend themselves against sinning. The most effective weapon against temptation and sin for Seripando was prayer, in particular the Lord's Prayer, which petitions God for one not to be led into temptation. Furthermore, he contended that in baptism the believer is prepared to battle against temptation in much the same way that a soldier or athlete prepares to meet his opponent. Just as the soldier first takes the standard of the army and, according to ancient custom, takes the military oath and then goes into combat, so too the Christian first takes the sign of the faith, namely baptism, in which he renounces the devil and his splendor, and then combats him and his armies. The Christian is also like the ancient athlete who first anoints himself and then wrestles with his adversary. In a similar fashion, the Christian must be cleansed with the holy anointing of chrism before going out to wrestle with the demon.[82]

Clearly Seripando does not take the possibility of temptation lightly. Yet, while he counsels his listeners to gird themselves for the struggle against sin, he sees temptation as a necessary and good thing because it gives the person who is undergoing the temptation the opportunity to praise God. Reflecting Saint Augustine's views of the necessity and worth of temptation, Seripando instructs the people of Salerno that without temptations individuals do not become better, nor do they make any gains toward salvation. Indeed, he states that without temptations no one would ever attain perfection nor be aware of his own strength to meet adversity. He concludes that without temptations no one enters into battle against the enemy; without fighting a battle, no one wins; without victory, no one is crowned. "Therefore, temptations are necessary so that we become better individuals, we acquire knowledge of ourselves, and we acquire the crown of life, fighting until death."[83]

Seripando's preoccupation with sin, temptation, and the need for self-transformation reflects a view of human nature that is Pauline and Augustinian in origin. This view of human nature emphasizes the corruption of humanity, its sinfulness, and its difficulty in doing good. This understanding of human nature is highlighted to emphasize the salvific work of Christ in the restoration of human nature to grace.[84] The result of this emphasis is the development of a theology and spirituality that is Christocentric in nature.

In his sermons on the Apostles' Creed, Seripando embodies this view of human nature. In the seventh sermon he informs the congregation that whenever the early Fathers thought about their conception and birth they were saddened because they recalled the filth and ugliness of sin with which they had come into the world.[85] Consequently, they cursed the day of their birth and the night of their conception because of the sin which had given rise to their being. While this might seem odd, Seripando asks:

> Tell me, when we are baptized, what else are we doing than cursing our first birth? Do we not renounce the demon of whom we are born servants? Do we not renounce his works and splendors, from which we are all naturally born, which even from our mother's womb we are inclined toward as a result of the natural defects and corruption of our deprived and contaminated nature?[86]

Therefore, Seripando instructs his flock to curse the day of their first birth, because they were born children of anger, and to bless the day of their second birth, that is, their baptism, because they were born children of grace. He explains:

> Let us curse our first birth, because we were born in sin; let us bless our second birth, because we emerged from the holy font pure and cleansed from every stain. Let us curse our first birth, because we were born members of Adam, a sinner and embezzler of God's law; let us bless our second birth, because we were born members of Christ, the just one who fulfilled perfectly God's law. Let us curse our first birth, because we were born children of Gehenna, of pain, and of eternal torment; let us bless our second birth, because we were reborn children of God, and full of hope of the inheritance of eternal life.[87]

Seripando illustrates how human nature, being born of the flesh, was subjugated to the desires of the flesh, always following its will. Consequently, humanity could not raise its mind to celestial thoughts and desires but was trapped by worldly and carnal thoughts. Humanity was born to eternal damnation, without hope of escaping God's wrath.[88] However, because of Christ's death and resurrection, the human race was no longer doomed to this fate. Seripando reminds the faithful that as a consequence of the blood of Christ the sinful nature of humanity was cleansed and purified.[89] Through baptism, every Christian becomes a member of Christ's body and shares in the effects of his salvific work, thereby freeing humanity from eternal damnation and providing the hope of eternal life. Christ died once for all and by his death destroyed all sins, so that after his resurrection he lives the life of God, alien to every fear of death. Therefore, the baptized must believe that, once they have received forgiveness of sins in baptism, they are dead to sin. For this reason, the day of baptism becomes for the Christian the day of rebirth and is a constant reminder of the perfection and transformation that each individual must strive for through the struggles and encounters with sin that accompany everyone throughout the journey of life. Baptism, then, becomes the foundation of the process of renewal and regeneration that Seripando encourages his listeners to undertake as he calls them to a spirit of repentance.

**COMMUNITY**

Because of the effects of Christ's death and resurrection and by virtue of baptism, every Christian shares in the same sonship of Jesus Christ, a relationship with God that gives an undying, eternal identity. Membership in the Church as the body of those who through baptism and the eucharist have acquired such an identity becomes the source of true spirituality. In this view, spirituality is an ecclesial experience.

Saint Paul taught that all members of the Church were in one way or another bearers of the Spirit. The gifts of the Spirit were shared by all, and therefore true Christian spirituality does not allow for discriminations that place one gift above the rest, since each member depends on the other. Therefore, the highest form of spirituality is relational. Neither Christian life nor human life itself is ever isolated existence. Humans are, by definition, social beings. To be human is to live in community. To be Christian is also to live in community, that is, the Church. To be spiritually Christian is to live always in relation with others, with one's brothers and sisters in the Body of Christ and in the human community at large.[90]

Seripando expresses these themes in several of his sermons on the Lord's Prayer. The relational aspect of Christian spirituality is evident in the first sermon, where he calls the Lord's Prayer the *Oratione Fraterna* "because in this prayer all Christians know and confess that they are brothers and sisters, since Christians do not ask for anything in this prayer for themselves which they do not ask for all other Christians as their brothers or sisters."[91] In the third sermon, Seripando continues this theme, adding the Pauline notion of the mystical body. He reminds his listeners that they are all members of one body through their common baptism and their relationship to each other under the headship of Christ.[92] However, he points out that this ideal is not present among the Christians of his day.

> And if you say that among Christians there exists estrangement, discord, war, which indicates that unity does not exist, as

you say, of this situation we must all feel sadness and weep, because it is a sign that we are not true, pure, and good Christians, since we are not one body as described by Saint Paul: we do not drink of that spirit which maintains, nourishes, and vivifies the virtues of this holy body: we are not the same thing in Christ, because we do not possess Christ, but rather our cupidity is our head. . . .[93]

Thus, Seripando admonishes his listeners to make Christ the cornerstone of this spiritual edifice and to cultivate the spiritual life by living with the other faithful in the unity of the Spirit.[94]

Given the social conditions that existed in Salerno at this time, Seripando hoped to raise his congregation's awareness that they were members of the same spiritual family. When the rule of Ferrante Sanseverino came to an end shortly before Seripando's arrival in Salerno, the peaceful relations that had existed among the various classes in the city began to break down as class animosities resurfaced.[95] Concerned with this situation, Seripando presented a striking denunciation of a class mentality that is contrary to a prayer that sees all as brothers and sisters born of one common Father:

I am amazed how the princes and great magnates do not remember each day in this prayer that their vassals are their brothers; and that the nobles do not remember that the commoners are their brothers; and that the wealthy do not think in saying this prayer that the poor are their brothers; and that the healthy do not realize that the infirm are their brothers; and that the learned do not see that the ignorant are their brothers because all say to the same Father "Pater Noster."[96]

Seripando's point here is to make the congregation aware of the ramifications of this prayer, which not only directs one to love God, but also to love one's neighbor, thereby building up the Christian community. By challenging each group to alter their way of life, Seripando hoped to foster a renewal, not only of the individual, but also of the Christian community and society.

## EUCHARIST

One of the means of building up the Christian community was the celebration of the eucharist. During the patristic age, the eucharist was understood as the event which brought together the people of God, not only to celebrate, but also to constitute the eschatological messianic community here and now. As such, it was the spiritual event par excellence, because it was the eschatological reality manifested and foreshadowed in history.[97] Furthermore, since the eucharistic mystery remains at the center of Christian life, there can be no renewal within religious society without returning to this banquet of love.[98]

The dominant influence on the formation of spirituality around the axis of the eucharist and the structure of the Church came from Ignatius of Antioch (d. ca. 110). He developed the view that salvation and spiritual or eternal life are realized and experienced through faithful communion in the eucharistic body of Christ. This body "formed" in the community of the Church brings together all the faithful under the leadership of the president of the eucharistic assembly, the bishop, surrounded by the college of presbyters and assisted by deacons. Ignatius insisted no one can claim a relationship with God giving eternal life unless there is constant interpretation in this eucharistic community.[99] The eucharist is crucial for spiritual life because it is crucial for the presence of the eschatological community here and now in history. Therefore, the eucharistic mysticism of Ignatius is basically biblical in that it maintains the eschatological orientation and the community basis that mark the biblical approach to spiritual life.[100]

A similar view is developed by Maximus the Confessor. For Maximus, spirituality becomes a matter of participation in the eucharistic community as a way of overcoming individualism through the purification of the heart from all passions and through the actual gathering of the eucharist, which places creation in the movement toward its proper eschatological end.[101]

Seripando also stresses the importance of the eucharist in his sermons and writings. Concerned with the heretical teachings of his day that denied that Christ was truly present in the eucharist, Seripando affirms Catholic doctrine that the bread and wine are truly the body and blood of Christ and not merely signs or symbols. He makes clear that Christ gave his body to his apostles and thus during the Mass Christ becomes actually present in the form of bread.[102] In the thirteenth sermon on the Lord's Prayer, Seripando expresses the patristic notion of the eucharist as unifying Christians into a community: "The third bread which is mentioned in scripture is the body of Our Lord Jesus Christ, found truly in the sacrament and sacrifice of the altar . . . which . . . unites the two peoples of the world, Hebrews and Gentiles."[103] He goes on to describe the eucharist as a "medicine" which transmits the effects of the death and resurrection of Christ and the forgiveness of sins.[104] This image of the eucharist as medicine is expressed by Ignatius of Antioch in his *Letter to the Ephesians*, where he describes the eucharist as "medicine of immortality, an antidote against death." The message in both Ignatius and Seripando is clear — the eucharist as "medicine" signifies that eternal life stems from participation, that is, reception of the eucharist, which Seripando exhorts his listeners to do on a regular, even daily,[105] basis since the eucharist heals the sick, strengthens the weak, and allows one to walk in the light of grace toward heavenly glory.[106]

Spirituality in this eucharistic context acquires a moral, psychological, and ontological context. The moral context rests on improving human nature and making it act and behave in a better way through moral achievement and virtue. By eating Christ's body, the individual will cultivate those virtues necessary for doing good works, which are the fruits of those sustained by this spiritual food.[107] Experiencing the fruits of the Spirit embodies the psychological context. By ontological is meant overcoming death through the acquisition of a new identity based on new relationships which are identical to the Father-Son relationship of the Holy Trinity. These three elements are found in Seripando's understanding of the relationship between the eucharist and the spiritual life:

> Do not love this world, nor the things which it offers you, but make yourselves experience a divine metamorphosis, transforming yourselves from within and renewing your minds with new and spiritual desires and love of heavenly things and of divine promises so that you may with taste and experience know what the will of God is towards you.[108]

The ontological context is expressed when Seripando, following the thought of Saint Augustine, states: ". . . this bread is granted to you not for the happiness of this temporal life, but of eternal life, because in this bread is concealed all of the hope of our spiritual life and of eternal blessedness."[109] The eucharist is, then, the sacred mystical meal and the food of spiritual life. Just as the carnal life needs food for sustenance, so too the spiritual life needs spiritual food to be perfected.[110] Since every day the individual dies spiritually, every day the individual needs this living bread, this bread of spiritual life in the same way as the body needs bread for nourishment. Through this spiritual food the life of the individual undergoes a metamorphosis which leads ultimately to the perfection of the spiritual life.[111]

The importance of the spiritual life, and thus its cultivation through participation in the eucharist, is made clear by Seripando in his distinguishing it from the carnal life. The carnal life is one that consents to, obeys, and serves sin, whereas the spiritual life resists, does not serve, and does not obey sin. One who strives for the spiritual life does everything possible to conquer sin. The individual living the carnal life, which is the life of the flesh, is led by his own desires and wishes, whereas the person who lives by the spirit is guided by God, following his will in everything. In the former, the individual seeks earthly treasures, whereas in the latter, heavenly treasures are sought.

Finally, the individual lives in himself in the carnal life, whereas in the spiritual life, the individual dies to himself, allowing Christ to live in him.[112] Thus, the faithful must live their lives in such a way that they may arrive at that eternal life in which one lives forever in happiness. This can be accomplished by incorporating the teachings of scripture into one's life, by performing good works, and by living according to the precepts of the faith.[113] Above all, one must receive the eucharist daily. Seripando makes this clear in the thirteenth sermon on the Lord's Prayer: "Every day we have need of this living bread, of this bread of the spiritual life.... Receive it, receive it every day so that each day you may profit from its reception."[114] Like Augustine, Seripando criticized the infrequent reception of the eucharist, stating that those who were not worthy to partake of this spiritual food daily were not worthy to partake of it once a year either.[115] In order to cultivate the spiritual life the individual was compelled to live and act in such a way as to be worthy always to receive Christ in the eucharist. Seripando believed that in this way, not only would each individual Christian's life be transformed and renewed, but so too the life of the community. Thus, during his episcopacy he encouraged the faithful to receive the eucharist daily as a means of restoring their spiritual and religious life.

## UNION WITH GOD

The cultivation of the spiritual life not only requires the frequent reception of communion and active participation in the eucharistic community. It also involves abandoning the things of this world, which then frees one to move toward union with God. Certainly the blessed life can be attained only after death, by a return to humanity's origin. But, in a certain sense, one can be said to be happy even now if one walks the right road to the blessed life and is filled with such a desire for the highest good that one would rather rise to it today. Since the soul comes from God and is divine, it strives to return to God. The love of God gives rise to this desire, according to Seripando.[116] This notion becomes the axis of his theological system. The soul ascends in steps to the knowledge of God and rests only when it has found its origin. However, knowledge of God is not possible without a prior moral cleansing.

For humanists, the purpose of Christian devotion was "an ever closer relationship and finally union with God. It was of the essence of humanist spirituality that it understood Christianity . . . as the development of an ever-deepening relationship first to God and then, through him, to other persons."[117] This relationship resulted not from any human effort but solely from divine initiative. Seripando reflects this view of God in his sermons, where the end of the spiritual life is union with God. This union with God is the natural result of one's belief in and love of God, which impels one to walk toward God, placing all one's hope in God.[118] To walk toward God means to make God the end of all one's thoughts, of all one's desires, of all one's labors.[119] Furthermore, this love of God entails not loving the things of this world. In his fourth sermon on the Apostles' Creed Seripando develops this idea: "He who truly believes in God never stands still, but walks toward God. He who walks toward God needs to separate himself from this world."[120] The individual who sincerely believes in God abandons the world, along with all its power, wisdom, and riches, confiding in God alone.[121]

Seripando further develops this theme in his fourth sermon on the Lord's Prayer. He states that the souls of the faithful desire to unite perfectly with God and to see God face to face.[122] This can be attained not only through external observances, but also through interior transformation, always guided by the divine initiative. In a letter to Marcantonio Flaminio, Seripando writes: "I imagine that almighty God always moves all of humanity, not only the elect, toward him, since he is the goal of all. . . . This movement is not only external through scripture and preaching, but more so internal through good thoughts and inspirations."[123] This inner renewal of the self, as one makes one's way toward God, transforms the lover into the loved as the believer achieves union with God.

## SERMONS TO THE CHILDREN OF SALERNO

Seripando's intention to foster a renewal of one's life toward a more Christian way of living, thereby leading to the reform of the Church and society through the preaching of sermons, is most evident in the special attention given to children in the sermons on the Lord's Prayer. Seripando desired to have young people, in particular children, present when he preached. This is evident in the first sermon on the Lord's Prayer:

> I desire at these lessons young boys and young girls whose souls are less corrupted than yours already grown old in and accustomed to a less than Christian way of life. For that reason, the schoolteacher Maestro Gabriele will ensure that his students come to these lessons in order that they will understand those words which each day they are obliged to recite.[124]

While it may at first appear unusual that the archbishop enjoins the schoolteacher to bring his pupils to the cathedral, in light of the aim of Seripando's reform program, along with the educational climate of Renaissance Italy, one is not surprised. Seripando's pastoral program strove for the regeneration of Christian life, which could be accomplished, among other means, through instruction. Seripando understood that the renewal of the manner of living, in a Christian sense, of the people had to have its beginnings in the education of young boys and girls.[125] However, by the year 1300 the Church had relinquished much of its educational role in Italy, resulting in a primary and secondary educational system that was secular in orientation.[126] As a result, catechism schools, or schools of Christian doctrine, that met on Sundays and religious holidays were organized. The purpose of these schools is evident from a popular expression which stated that these schools taught students "the holy fear of God, to read, to write, and to count on the abacus."[127] Clearly the aim of these schools was to impart religious instruction, along with rudimentary reading and writing, to ignorant and middle- and lower-class children.[128] Given the secular nature of Renaissance education in Italy and Seripando's own understanding of the role of education in the formation and renewal of Christian life, it is likely that the schoolteacher to whom Seripando refers taught either at one of the catechism schools in the city or at the local parish.[129] Seripando's request that the schoolteacher bring his students to hear the sermons reflects his tireless efforts to ensure that the children of Salerno receive not only an academic education but also religious instruction. Seripando believed that children needed to be instructed so as to allow for a better understanding of cultural and social phenomena. In addition, they needed to be educated in Christian ethics so as to raise the moral foundation upon which to create a more diligent Christian society.[130]

Seripando's wish to have children present among the congregation and the constant attention and references made to them in the course of his sermons do not simply indicate the pedagogical nature of these sermons. More importantly, the presence of children contributes to and illustrates the overall aim of Seripando's pastoral reform program — the regeneration of the Christian life and the salvation of the souls entrusted to his care. Seripando placed his hope for the renewal of Christian living in Salerno with the children of that city. Here too there is a link between Seripando's request and the aim of the schools of Christian doctrine. The reason Catholic reformers established such schools was not only to provide rudimentary religious instruction, but also to help individuals live better lives and thereby attain salvation in the life to come. Thus, the desire to reform morals and save souls motivated the educational program of these schools.[131] This common goal of the schools of Christian doctrine and Seripando's preaching is apparent in his second sermon on the Lord's Prayer:

> Let me say a few words to these children, who because of my orders have come to hear the Word of God, because I must render an account to God no less of them than of you, and to tell you the truth, my hope in seeing in Salerno some form of renewal and some true light of Christian life is more in them than in you others who are older, because they are less contaminated and mixed up in the affairs of this world than you are.[132]

Concerned with the spiritual well-being of the youth of Salerno, Seripando points out how so many are tempted by worldliness. They have become enamored with the beauty of the body, they desire fame in the ostentation of worldly possessions, they despise the old and the powerless. To such young people the commandments of Christ are like poison, while the food presented to them by the devil is sweet. Seripando blames the parents for the circumstances of the youth. In his seventeenth sermon on the Lord's Prayer, he indicates that children do not know the doctrines of the faith because parents have "immersed their children in a pagan life and in the appetites of the flesh."[133] In a later sermon he picks up this theme, indicating that parents teach their children the doctrines of this world, teaching them to love the goods of secular society, rather than to love Jesus Christ.[134] These remarks seem to suggest Seripando's perception of hedonistic values and a lack of solidarity in Salerno.

Addressing the children, Seripando asks why they are tempted to live a life of worldliness. For him, the answer is simple: "We see many times the bad and pernicious customs of the father, the mother, the brothers, of the entire household. We see little piety, little faith, few examples of Christian life. This is a great temptation because the devil speaks in your ears and says, 'Do you want to be better than your elders? Do as they do.' "[135] Consequently, Seripando censures the youth for living as friends rather than enemies of the devil, acting not as Christians, but as infidels.[136] For him, the poor example of adults had already begun to corrupt the children of Salerno.

To correct this situation, Seripando reminds both parents and godparents of their responsibility to teach their children the rudiments of the faith. He urges the parents to teach their children the Apostles' Creed and the Lord's Prayer, which summarize the basic truths of the faith.[137] Similarly, he pleads with the godparents that they constantly remind their godchildren when they come of age of the baptismal promises made in their name:

> My child, in your name I renounced the demon and the works and splendor of the demon, which are the three things that send us into exile, banishing us from the kingdom of Christ. The demon is the adversary of Christ and the enemy of human salvation who never ceases with a variety of temptations to separate us from faith in Christ. His works are all of the movements with which he attempts that we do our own will and not the will of Christ. His splendors are all of the goods and grandeurs of this world which he promises to give us.[138]

Concerned, then, with the bad example of parents which leads children astray, Seripando calls on the youth to follow the example of their heavenly Father rather than that of their earthly parents, so that the actions of their lives would lead to their salvation.

## CONCLUSION

The sermons of Girolamo Seripando as archbishop of Salerno provide a clear testimony of the moral and religious problems manifested in the lives of the people of Salerno in the sixteenth century.[139] Without hesitation Seripando proposed the formation and renewal of the manner of life of his flock along truly Christian principles. It was his hope that his reform program would result in an increase in faith and religious piety among those who professed to be Catholic, with particular attention placed on the youth of the diocese. As we have seen, because he placed such hope for religious renewal on the young people of Salerno, Seripando firmly exhorted them to attend the catechetical and doctrinal lessons, which he considered especially important for spiritual formation. His sermons mirror the fervor and intensity of the Catholic reformers of the sixteenth century, with their emphasis on asceticism, mysticism, piety, devotion, charity, and prayer as a means of fostering a renewal of the spiritual life of the faithful.

The themes expressed by Seripando in his sermons reflect his spiritual life and thought. For him, the help of souls was the principal aim of his preaching. Consequently, his sermons bear witness to a proponent of the renewal of religious and spiritual life based upon moral and religious values, scripture and the Church Fathers, most especially Paul and Augustine. Based on scriptural and patristic themes and on his own personal devotion, Seripando's sermons spoke to the practical spiritual needs of his listeners. He hoped and desired to move the listener to lead a better Christian life. In this way he revived the scriptural sermon preached in the spirit of the Fathers that aimed at reaching "men and women by persuading them, preaching to the heart and touching their will."[140]

The renewal that Seripando advocated did not imply a repudiation of traditional dogma, liturgical practices, and ecclesiastical hierarchy, nor did it threaten to disrupt the unity of the Church. His reform program, which was in many respects humanist in orientation, reflected his desire for purification. This type of reform emerged from his desire to return to the primitive evangelical ideals and corresponded with the various currents within the Church of his day that worked toward the moral, intellectual, and spiritual reform of the institution and its members. Seripando hoped not only to teach doctrine through his sermons, but also to correct the customs and habits of the people. Consequently, his preaching was an integral part of his vast program to reform the diocese of Salerno.

## NOTES

1. Hubert Jedin, *Papal Legate at the Council of Trent, Cardinal Seripando*, trans. Frederic C. Eckhoff (St. Louis: B. Herder Book Co., 1947), 524.
2. Antonio Balducci, *Girolamo Seripando: Arcivescovo di Salerno, 1554-1563* (Cava dei Tirreni: Arti Grafiche di Mauro, 1963), 52.
3. Jedin, *Papal Legate*, 525.
4. Ibid., 526.
5. Of these sermons, only the series on the Apostles' Creed and the Lord's Prayer are extant.
6. David Gutiérrez, "Hieronymi Seripandi 'Diarium de Vita Sua' (1513-1562)," *Analecta Augustiniana* 26 (1963).
7. Rocchina M. Abbondanza, *Girolamo Seripando tra Evangelismo e Riforma Cattolica* (Naples: Ferraro, 1982), 72.
8. Jedin, *Papal Legate*, 538.
9. Donato Dente, *Salerno nel Seicento: Nell'Interno di una città, vol. 2, pt. 1: Inediti per la Storia Civile e Religiosa* (Salerno: Edisud, 1993), 305.
10. Abbondanza, 80.
11. Donato Dente, *Salerno nel Seicento: Nell'Interno di una città, vol. 1: Istituzioni Culturali* (Salerno: Edisud, 1990), xxv.
12. Frederick J. McGinness, "Preaching Ideals and Practice in Counter-Reformation Rome," *The Sixteenth Century Journal 11 (1980)*: 119.
13. John W. O'Malley, "Content and Rhetorical Forms in Sixteenth Century Treatises on Preaching," in *Renaissance Eloquence: Studies in the Theory and Practice of Renaissance Rhetoric*, ed. James J. Murphy (Berkeley: University of California Press, 1983), 240. See also John W. O'Malley, *Praise and Blame in Renaissance Rome* (Durham: Duke University Press, 1979), 43.
14. Ibid.
15. This aim of the preacher reflects the duties of the orator as described by Cicero. See McGinness, 117. Also see Frederick J. McGin-

ness, *Right Thinking and Sacred Oratory in Counter-Reformation Rome* (Princeton: Princeton University Press, 1995), 55.

16. McGinness, *Right Thinking*, 55.
17. O'Malley, "Content and Rhetorical Forms," 244.
18. John W. O'Malley, "Erasmus and the History of Sacred Rhetoric: The Ecclesiastes of 1535," *Erasmus of Rotterdam Society Yearbook* 5 (1985): 14.
19. John W. O'Malley, "Form, Content and Influence of Works About Preaching Before Trent: The Franciscan Contribution," in *I Frati Minori tra '400 e '500: Atti del XII Convegno Internazionale, Assisi, 18-20 Ottobre 1984* (Assisi: Centro di Studi Francescani, 1986), 49.
20. Larissa Taylor, *Soldiers of Christ: Preaching in Late Medieval and Reformation France* (New York: Oxford University Press, 1992), 84.
21. Ibid., 101.
22. O'Malley, "Content and Rhetorical Forms," 246.
23. Christophor of Padua, *Canones Verbi Dei Concionatoribus Ordinis Fratrum Eremitarum S. Augustini* (Rome, 1555), 4, no. 7. For a discussion of the significance of this instruction in the new approach to preaching see McGinness, *Right Thinking*, 37-38.
24. Ibid., no. 6.
25. Ibid., no. 16.
26. O'Malley, "Content and Rhetorical Forms," 248-49.
27. Ibid.
28. Ronald F.E. Weissman, "Sacred Eloquence: Humanist Preaching and Lay Piety in Renaissance Florence," in *Christianity and the Renaissance: Image and Religious Imagination in the Quattrocento*, eds. Timothy Verdon and John Henderson (Syracuse: Syracuse University Press, 1990), 261.
29. McGinness, *Right Thinking*, 30. See also "Decree on Instruction and Preaching," Council of Trent, Session 5, no. 11 in *Decrees of the Ecumenical Councils*, 2 vols., ed. Norman P. Tanner (Washington, DC: Georgetown University Press, 1990), 2: 669.
30. Taylor, 141.
31. Abbondanza, 72. See also McGinness, *Right Thinking*, 35-36.
32. Jedin, *Papal Legate*, 531.
33. PS, 41.
34. PRS, sermon 16.
35. Abbondanza, 64.
36. Biblioteca Statale Angelica, Rome, MSS 780, f. 1.
37. PRS, 98-9.
38. Taylor, 150.
39. Massimo Petrocchi, *Storia della Spiritualità Italiana*, 2 vols. (Rome: Edizioni di Storia e Letteratura, 1978), 1: 127-28. See also P. Pourrat, *Christian Spirituality*, 3 vols. (London: Burns Oates and Washbourne, 1927), 230.

40. Agostino Trapé, "Il principio fondamentale della spiritualità Agostiniana e la vita monastica," *Sanctus Augustinus Vitae Spiritualis Magister* (Rome: Analecta Augustiniana, 1959), 1.
41. Ibid., 2-3.
42. Ibid., 37-38.
43. PRS, 104.
44. Ibid.
45. BNN, MSS COD VIII, vol. 26, f. 37r.
46. PRS, 240-41.
47. These ideas are expressed in the ninth and tenth sermons on the Lord's Prayer.
48. PRS, 187.
49. PS, 42.
50. PRS, 149.
51. Ibid.
52. Angelo Penna, "Lo Studio della Bibbia nella spiritualità di S. Agostino," *Sanctus Augustinus Vitae Spiritualis Magister* (Rome: Analecta Augustiniana, 1959), 152.
53. James D. Tracy, "Ad Fontes: The Humanist Understanding of Scripture as Nourishment for the Soul," in *Christian Spirituality: High Middle Ages and Reformation*, ed. Jill Raitt (New York: Crossroad, 1987), 254.
54. PRS, 206.
55. Ibid., 210-11.
56. Ibid., 206.
57. Ibid., 212.
58. Ibid., 211.
59. "Seripando an den Fürsten von Salerno über göttliches Vorherwissen und Willensfreiheit," in Hubert Jedin, *Girolamo Seripando Sein Leben und Denken im Geisteskampf des 16 Jahrunderts* (Wurzburg: Rita Verlag, 1937), 469.
60. PRS, 214.
61. William J. Bouwsma, "The Spirituality of Renaissance Humanism," in *Christian Spirituality: High Middle Ages and Reformation*, ed. Jill Raitt (New York: Crossroad, 1987), 240.
62. Daniel E. Bornstein, *The Bianchi of 1399: Popular Devotion in Late Medieval Italy* (Ithaca: Cornell University Press, 1993), 34-35.
63. Leon E. Halkin, "La piété d'Erasme," *Révue de l'Histoire des Religions* 79 (1984): 695.
64. *Dictionnaire de Spiritualité*, 14 vols. to date (Paris: Beuchesne, 1936-1990), 14: 660.
65. PRS, 152.
66. Ibid.
67. Ibid., 153.
68. PRS, 91-92.

69. PRS, 230.
70. Ibid.
71. Ibid.
72. Ibid., 231.
73. Ibid., 232.
74. PS, 292.
75. Ibid., 166.
76. Ibid., 309.
77. Ibid., 310.
78. PRS, 268.
79. Ibid., 269.
80. Ibid., 148.
81. Ibid., 293-94.
82. Ibid., 293.
83. Ibid., 294.
84. Gino Ciolini, "Scrittori spirituali Agostiniani dei secoli XIV e XV in Italia," *Sanctus Augustinus Vitae Spiritualis Magister* (Rome: Analecta Augustiniana, 1959), 340.
85. PS, 119.
86. Ibid., 121.
87. Ibid.
88. Ibid., 127-28.
89. Ibid., 122.
90. John D. Zizioulas, "The Early Christian Community," in *Christian Spirituality: Origins to the Twelfth Century*, eds. Bernard McGinn, John Meyendorff, Jean Leclercq (New York: Crossroad, 1985), 28-31.
91. PRS, 93.
92. Ibid., 114.
93. Ibid., 113.
94. Ibid., 240.
95. Dente, *Inediti per la Storia*, 294.
96. Ibid., 93.
97. Zizioulas, 29.
98. Petrocchi, 1: 130.
99. Zizioulas, 31.
100. Ibid., 32.
101. Ibid., 43.
102. BNN, MSS COD VIII, AA, vol. 26, f. 130v.
103. PRS, 224.
104. Ibid., 226.
105. Ibid., 223; 227.
106. Ibid., 229.
107. BNN, MSS COD VIII, AA, vol. 26, f. 129v-130r.
108. PRS, 203.

109. Ibid., 226-27.
110. BNN, MSS COD VIII, AA, vol. 22, f. 286v.
111. BNN, MSS COD VIII, AA, vol. 22, f. 286r.
112. BNN, MSS COD VIII, AA, vol. 26, f. 159r-160v.
113. PRS, 97.
114. Ibid., 224-27.
115. Ibid., 227. As Bornstein points out, despite the Fourth Lateran Council's (1215) requirement that the faithful receive communion at least once a year, in late medieval Italy few chose to communicate more frequently and others communicated even less often. Such infrequent reception of communion continued into the early modern period as well. See Bornstein, 13.
116. Biblioteca Statale Angelica, Rome, MSS 780, f. 1.
117. Bouwsma, 243-44.
118. PS, 68.
119. Ibid., 56.
120. Ibid., 78-79.
121. Ibid., 59.
122. PRS, 125-26.
123. BNN, MSS COD VIII, AA, vol. 22, f. 10.
124. PRS, 92.
125. Donato Dente, "Vita culturale ed istituzioni scolastiche a Salerno nel Cinquecento: Note e Documenti," in *Salerno e il Principato Citra nell'età moderna (secoli XVI-XIX)*, ed. Francesco Sofia (Naples: Edizioni Scientifiche Italiane, 1987), 853.
126. Paul F. Grendler, *Schooling in Renaissance Italy: Literacy and Learning, 1300-1600* (Baltimore: The Johns Hopkins University Press, 1989), 41.
127. Dente, *Istituzioni culturali*, 57.
128. Grendler, 359.
129. Dente, "Vita culturale," 826.
130. Dente, *Inediti per la Storia*, 296.
131. Grendler, 332.
132. PRS, 94.
133. Ibid., 261.
134. Ibid., 292.
135. Ibid.
136. PS, 137.
137. PRS, 91.
138. PS, 136.
139. Dente, *Istituzioni culturali*, 677.
140. McGinness, *Right Thinking*, 49.

**Chapter Five**

# THE REFORMS IN SALERNO

Girolamo Seripando was among the leading proponents of Catholic reform in the sixteenth century. He worked tirelessly to extirpate the abuses that had developed over the years within the Church that made it the object of criticism both from the Protestants and those who remained within the institution. Faced with the many problems and abuses that plagued the Church, many reformers desired to return to the apostolic model found in the scriptures. "Primitivism — the desire to return to some pristine apostolic model — was directly linked to concerns that pastoral duties were not being properly fulfilled in the contemporary church. The preachers' critical comments and their attempts to reform their secular and religious confreres must therefore be understood within the context of their zeal to make the church conform to the early apostolic ideal."[1] Seripando is no exception here. In his introductory sermon to the cycle on the Lord's Prayer, he divides the history of the Church into four ages: the golden age, representing the primitive apostolic Church; the silver age, representing the patristic era; the bronze age, encompassing the medieval Church; and the age of lead, referring to his contemporary Church.[2] Having characterized the Church's history in this way, Seripando indicated his hope for the Church, shared by many of the reformers of the day: "Many times I have thought and desired to see our Christian and Catholic Church in only one way, leaving aside all other things, similar to that first very poor and very holy Church."[3]

## CONDITIONS IN THE DIOCESE OF SALERNO

Seripando was not ignorant of the state of his diocese when he arrived as its archbishop in 1554. He had made frequent visits to the city as prior general of the Augustinians, as well as to the court of Ferrante Sanseverino during his reign as Prince of Salerno. Although these visits gave him some insight into the conditions in the city and the diocese, he had scarcely any knowledge of the details. When he arrived in Salerno, Seripando found conditions in need of improvement, both spiritually and materially. First and foremost he concerned himself with the spiritual decay into which the city had lapsed. Many of the clergy and laity had failed to observe ecclesiastical discipline or good customs. Seripando hoped to inaugurate a reform that would restore the clergy and the laity to their ancient dignity and religiosity.[4]

The diocese of Salerno, which was comprised of 150 parishes, was suffering economically. Given the modest economic state of the population, especially in the rural areas of the diocese, many of the churches were physically neglected and in need of repair. Some churches, for example, had no roofs. This situation was not limited to the rural churches but also applied to some in the city.[5] Clerical income was also extremely low. A survey of the incomes of eighty parish priests taken during a pastoral visitation in 1511 bears this out. Of these eighty priests only one earned thirty ducats a year, two earned twenty-four ducats, five earned twenty ducats, two earned eighteen ducats, eight earned fifteen ducats, six earned twelve ducats, twenty earned ten ducats, and the remaining thirty-six earned between nine and three ducats a year.[6] It was difficult to live on such incomes, and this situation had not improved by the time of Seripando's appointment as archbishop.

A similar situation existed within the monastic communities. For example, the nuns of the Order of Saint Clare lived "in greatest poverty" ("*in maxima paupertate*"). When the abbess of the Benedictine nuns in Eboli was appointed, she was unable to pay Rome the fees attached to the bull of nomination at the time of her appointment. That the economic situation within monastic communities, in particular female communities, did not improve is seen by the efforts made to reduce expenses by limiting the number of monks or nuns that were accepted into the community.[7]

The economic conditions grew worse, as we have already discussed, by the mid-sixteenth century.[8] Seripando found a church not only in spiritual disrepair but in material ruin as well. In a letter to Augusto Cocciano just two weeks after his arrival in Salerno, he wrote: "Here they are lacking everything for divine worship and for the material renovation of the buildings which are all in ruin."[9] In fact, Seripando not only found the cathedral in need of repair, but also the episcopal palace, which was in such a state of ruin that he was unable to live there.[10] These conditions impacted the religious life of the diocese and compelled Seripando to address these economic problems. Yet, despite these concerns, he knew that his first obligation was to the spiritual needs of the faithful entrusted to his care, and it was in this area that he spent most of his time and energy.

At the time of Seripando's nomination as archbishop of Salerno, the religious life of the diocese was regulated by the synodal constitutions promulgated in 1484 by Archbishop Giovanni d'Aragona. Because the provisions of these constitutions were still at the heart of Salerno's religious life at the outset of his episcopacy, they provide a glimpse of the social and religious problems that were prevalent in Salerno not only in the final decades of the fifteenth century, but also as late as the mid-sixteenth century.[11] Many of the problems dealt with in these constitutions, which regulated the life of the faithful and especially the life of the clergy, were ones that Seripando himself had to contend with when he became archbishop of Salerno.

After issuing prescriptions against heretics and schismatics, as well as against those who assisted the Turks in their frequent incursions along the coast of Salerno, the constitutions deal with the most common vices found among the people that needed correction. Among the bad habits singled out were blasphemy, concubinage, superstitious beliefs, usury, sorcery, and immorality within marriages. The constitutions also established a time frame within which parents were to have their children baptized and limited the number of godfathers a child could have at the time of baptism. Concerned with the manner in which the laity observed religious holidays, the constitutions also issued regulations on the relationship between work and holidays.[12]

The constitutions called the clergy to live a more austere and disciplined life and to conduct themselves in a manner that reflected their religious state. The constitutions issued prescriptions that renewed the requirement to wear a distinctive habit and the tonsure; reminded the clergy of the prohibition to be absent from the diocese without permission; warned against procuring sacred orders through the mediation of the laity; forbade the clergy from living with women and participating in games of chance or card playing; and admonished the clergy not to carry arms and not to wander through taverns.[13] The constitutions also condemned one of the most widespread abuses of the period, the accumulation of multiple benefices and the subsequent failure to reside in one's parish.[14]

While these constitutions served as a guide for the pastoral visitations conducted during the first half of the sixteenth century, the reports from those visitations indicate that in reality the constitutions made little, if any, impact on the religious situation in Salerno. In fact, it seems that the vast majority of the clergy were not even knowledgeable about the regulations found in the constitutions.[15] Indeed, despite the condemnations and efforts to renew the spiritual climate of Salerno through the prescriptions found in these constitutions, the moral and religious life of the clergy and laity had not changed when Seripando arrived in Salerno seventy years after d'Aragona had promulgated the constitutions.

## SERIPANDO'S REFORM PROGRAM

Seripando immediately began to make preparations for a reform initiative. During the four-month period between his consecration and possession of the diocese (May to September 1554), he began drawing up guidelines for a diocesan synod.[16] At the same time he realized that his authority in implementing reform was limited since he had no jurisdiction over the many exempt clergy, secular and religious, in the diocese. A number of the clergy profited from their exempt status by giving themselves to luxurious living and to other activities that were prohibited, leading to a decline in the observance of their religious life and giving rise to scandal. Recognizing this, Pope Julius III issued a brief, *Magnitudo meritorum*, to Seripando on 15 August 1554 which gave him jurisdiction to visit, reform, and punish those clerics who enjoyed exemption from episcopal jurisdiction.[17] Ready to implement a reform program, eight days after his arrival in Salerno, Seripando convened the cathedral chapter, announcing to them his desire to institute reform in the diocese as quickly as possible.

Besides his concern for a spiritual regeneration, Seripando was also confronted, as we have seen, with a diocese in need of physical renovation. The economic crisis into which the city had been thrust with the departure of Ferrante Sanseverino did not spare the diocese. In a letter to Cocciano, Seripando alluded to the "ruins of the Church" (*"rovine della Chiesa"*) in Salerno.[18] Far more revealing is Seripando's letter to the holy Roman Emperor, Charles V, in which he asks for the emperor's financial assistance to address the material problems within the diocese. Seripando explains that he is writing to the emperor to describe the terrible physical conditions he found in the diocese and to petition his help in restoring the churches in the diocese to a better state.[19] Providing Charles V with some examples, Seripando describes the cathedral, which he characterizes as one of the most beautiful in Italy, as being reduced to such ruin due to years of neglect. He describes the episcopal palace as being uninhabitable, thereby forcing him to live in a rented house. In addition to the physical deterioration of many of the churches in Salerno, Seripando indicates that some parishes had been so impoverished that they did not even possess those things necessary for the celebration of liturgy, such as vestments.[20] Given these burdens which were afflicting the church of Salerno, Seripando calls the emperor's financial assistance a "work of piety" (*"opera di pietà"*). He indicates that he makes this request because of the emperor's religious spirit and desire to preserve and increase the liturgical life of the church. He assures Charles V that the reputation of Salerno will increase and be known by all because of his generous assistance, which will be remembered forever.[21]

Seripando's efforts and labors in the physical restoration of the church of Salerno from the damage which through the years had resulted from various calamities and negligences were important and admirable. He was vigilant of and involved with all the efforts of renovation. Consequently, the diocese was able to rise from its material ruin. However, far more important to Seripando was the need to repair the church of Salerno from its spiritual ruins. Thus, despite the physical needs of the diocese, he did not allow that program to take precedence over or to dominate his religious reform efforts. Just two months after his arrival, Seripando opened a diocesan synod on 23 November

1554 aimed at reforming the church of Salerno and, in particular, improving clerical life, which was the most difficult task facing him.

The 138 constitutions that resulted reveal Seripando's burden and anxiety in introducing reform. Among the most important constitutions, marked by a spirit of vigorous and courageous reform, were twenty-six regulating the choral office, twenty-two concerning the celebration of the Mass, seven dealing with confession and confessors, and nineteen restoring discipline and renewing female monastic communities.[22]

In his introductory letter to the synodal constitutions, Seripando spelled out the aims of this reform and his reasons for convening the synod. Indicating that he had been called by God to govern the spiritual life of the church in Salerno, it was his obligation to restore the liturgical life of the diocese, along with good and honest customs among the people and the clergy.[23] Seripando reminded all of the inhabitants of the diocese that there already existed synodal regulations which had for the most part been neglected. Consequently, he pointed out that many offenses had been committed against these regulations, as well as against clerical life and honesty and, far worse, against the commandments of Christian life. Given this situation, new regulations were needed, which account for his convening a synod and promulgating the constitutions. Seripando firmly warned that from the moment the constitutions were promulgated offenses would no longer be tolerated but would be severely punished. Seripando indicated that, springing from a paternal love, the castigations against abuses were meant to encourage a penitential spirit within the individual.[24] This penitential spirit, along with the reforms spelled out in the synodal constitutions themselves, would, he hoped, result in a meaningful renewal of the religious life of the diocese, the intent of the synod in the first place.

## THE DIOCESAN SYNOD

### REFORM OF CLERICAL LIFE

There were 342 priests in the diocese of Salerno when Seripando began his episcopacy, seventy-eight of whom were canons. The vast majority of these clerics were not true aspirants to the priesthood, but individuals who sought personal advantage from their clerical status (*clerici propter utilitatem*).²⁵ These clerics ranged in age from 30 to 70 and had acquired the clerical habit as children, continuing to wear it even after marrying. At various times in the past the archbishops had ordered these clerics to renounce their clerical garb, and hence status, in vain.²⁶ In his thirteenth sermon on the Apostles' Creed, Seripando provides a descriptive picture of the state of the clergy. He begins by asking whether the successors to the apostles and Fathers of the Church could be considered holy. He answers by pointing out how so many clerics are "full of ignorance and bad customs, of simony, of bad examples, addicted to excess eating or drinking, living in concubinage, swindlers, full of fraud, envy, loathsome to God and to all Christian people."²⁷ Seripando continued that among the clergy are seen grave sins and wicked dishonesty, which for the most part go unpunished and uncorrected.²⁸ Furthermore, Seripando was concerned with the widespread accumulation of multiple benefices in Salerno, as he indicated in a letter to Augusto Cocciano, writing that the people never see their parish priest, resulting in the collapse of both the spiritual and the temporal edifice of the Church.²⁹

Given this situation, Seripando realized his principal difficulties were the improvement of clerical training and the appointment of competent priests for the care of souls (*cura animarum*). He first sought to implement a personal reform among the clergy and to call them back to a consciousness of their state by the living out and fulfillment of the disciplinary norms of the Church.³⁰ Having then prepared the way with an initial pruning of the more apparent abuses, it would not be difficult to introduce gradually more incisive and extensive reforms.

Among Seripando's greatest concerns was the formation of priests, particularly intellectual, which had greatly declined. This was one of the consequences of the non-residency of the bishop, which contributed to the minimal level of cultural, intellectual, and spiritual preparation of the clergy in the sixteenth century. However, in Salerno there was a difference between rural and urban priests, the latter taking advantage of the opportunities of the city in which they found themselves. During the reign of Ferrante Sanseverino, when the cultural and intellectual life of Salerno flourished and studies were encouraged, the clergy, as well as candidates for the priesthood, had the opportunity to receive an adequate education.³¹ Furthermore, between 1535-1540 a school for the instruction and education of young boys was founded in the city. The income from certain benefices *sine cura* was transferred to this school in the hope that aspirants to the priesthood would avail themselves of this opportunity.[32] However, when Sanseverino's reign came to an end in Salerno, so too did the climate that supported and encouraged the intellectual and cultural formation of the clergy.

While educational opportunities existed for the urban clergy, that was not true for the clergy who served in the rural regions of the diocese. Here, where little formal education was available, aspirants to the priesthood were entrusted either to a priest with some educational background or to a local schoolteacher to receive rudimentary schooling. Consequently, the cultural background of the rural clergy, even in the care of souls, was quite basic and highly insufficient.[33]

To address this situation was among the aims of the diocesan synod. Seripando's main concern was to provide the faithful with competent clerics who would provide an example of holiness to those to whom they ministered. The synodal decrees were meant to assist Seripando in this task by restoring the pastoral duties of the clergy, his chief concern being the *cura animarum*. In order to assess the situation within the diocese, he sought to draw up a register that listed the names of the clergy and summarized the state of the clergy within the diocese. This would allow the archbishop to know "those whom we have as coadjutors in our ministry and whom, if necessary, we can make use of without offending our conscience, in the care of souls, and other ecclesiastical ministries."[34]

To accomplish this, Seripando first acquainted himself personally with the clergy of the diocese. He ordered all priests to meet with him within one year of the publication of the synodal decrees or be deprived of the fruits of their benefices.[35] Seripando wished to acquaint himself with his clergy so as to be certain that worthy priests ministered to the faithful. To ensure good priests for the future, the synodal constitutions also established prescriptions for candidates for Holy Orders. All candidates were to be presented to the archbishop by worthy men whom he knew and who had knowledge of the candidate's learning, habits, age, and those things necessary for promotion to the clerical state.[36] Furthermore, one month prior to ordination, each candidate was to present himself to the archbishop and remain with him for three days so that "we can know and examine those things which are possible to be known and examined, so that we do not too quickly, and without due consideration, impose our hands in ordination against the precept of the apostle Paul."[37] These decrees, along with the prescription that priests could not celebrate their first Mass without an express license from the archbishop himself,[38] were meant to eliminate those pernicious abuses and many evils that were prevalent among the clergy in the diocese at the time of his arrival.

Seripando was also concerned with the quality of confessors in Salerno. Until he became acquainted with the priests in his diocese, the synodal constitutions decreed that all those who had the license to hear confession would be permitted to continue to do so.[39] In the meantime, the constitutions ordered that all confessors who lived in the city of Salerno, within one month of the publication of these constitutions, and those confessors who lived in the rural regions, within two months, were to present themselves to the archbishop "so that we can come to know them. Those that we find most suitable, we will assign with a written license to hear confessions, given to them free and without payment."[40] Once the archbishop has chosen the confessors for the diocese, no one else could lawfully appoint a priest as a confessor who was not among those accepted by the archbishop, under the penalty of excommunication. In addition, any priest who had not been chosen by the archbishop could not lawfully hear the confession of others under the pain of excommunication.[41]

Concerned with the way confessors administered the sacrament of penance, as well as with the effects of confession on the penitent, Seripando prohibited confessors from imposing monetary penances, even if the revenues from such penances were to be used for the good of the Church or other pious works. Such penances did not have a spiritual benefit on the individual, nor did they move one toward an inner renewal or transformation. To accomplish this goal, Seripando suggested that the confessor impose a regimen of prayer, fasting, and almsgiving as a penance, according to the seriousness of the sins.[42] Such a penance, more in line with the theological understanding of the sacrament of penance, would assist in the spiritual regeneration and reform of the individual.

As already seen, scripture held an important place in Seripando's spirituality. The centrality of scripture was linked with the seriousness with which he took the obligation to preach. While this obligation was first and foremost the responsibility of the bishop, it also belonged to the secular clergy who had regular contact with the faithful. However, when Seripando came to Salerno, he discovered that only a small number of the secular clergy possessed sufficient knowledge and training to preach. As a result of this situation, the clergy were no longer fulfilling their duty to preach or to teach the faithful. Seripando alludes to this situation in his twelfth sermon on the Lord's Prayer. He indicates that the explanation of the scriptures occurs on rare occasions and, consequently, the faithful are not fed with the bread of God's word. He asks, "How difficult would it be if every day in the Church fifty words were said simply without much arrogance, without much fineness, according to what the Holy Spirit dictated?"[43]

Given this deficiency on the part of the clergy, the synodal constitutions attempt to rectify the situation. The constitutions prescribe that all priests who have the care of souls must preach every Sunday and feast day. The object of their preaching should be the explanation of the gospel.[44] Additionally, in their preaching, the clergy should instruct the people in the truths of the faith, the importance of observing fasts and giving alms, and exhort them to pray to the Blessed Virgin Mary. They should urge the faithful to confess themselves and to receive communion frequently.[45] The constitutions also specify that the clergy should use the sermon to admonish the faithful that they should pardon offenses committed against them and to teach their flock how to comport themselves at the liturgy. In terms of the latter, they should be taught

> how to listen to the Mass with reverence, how to adore the host, how to raise their minds to heaven while the secret prayer is said and during the Sanctus; and that they beat their breasts when the Agnus Dei is recited, that upon hearing the name of Jesus Christ they always bow their head or make another sign of reverence.[46]

By faithfully carrying out this obligation, the clergy would provide the laity with sound Christian teaching, counsel, and practical suggestions that would allow for personal regeneration, leading toward the living out of the Christian life.[47]

Seripando believed that the clergy should not only preach the Word, but they should also teach by example. This required reforming their way of life by recalling them to the dignity of the customs of their lifestyle. Seripando intended that the example of the clergy not create any obstacles in the renewal of the faithful. These two hopes were the object of the synodal constitutions that dealt with the lifestyle of the clergy. Concerning the overall behavior of the clergy the constitutions state: "We order in virtue of holy obedience all priests and clergy of whatever state, rank, and condition that they must in all their bodily gestures, in their walking, principally in their talk, and in their eyes always demonstrate modesty and honesty."[48] The constitutions further specify the type of behavior that was considered appropriate for the clergy. Such behavior as excess eating and drinking, immodest acts, quarrels, and animosity was intolerable among the clergy and were forbidden not only in the scriptures, but also by the saints and general councils.[49] Furthermore, as had already been prohibited by the general councils, the synodal constitutions restated the prescriptions against dancing, attending theatrical presentations, and living with women.[50] In addition, Seripando desired that the clergy set a good example for the faithful by fasting, performing works of mercy, and worthily celebrating the sacraments.[51]

In order for the clergy to provide the faithful with a good example, it was necessary that they be present among the people. As a result, Seripando imposed the observance of residency on those clerics who were entrusted with parishes, since he believed this obligation to be one of the most efficacious ways to reform the Church. Concerning residence, the synodal constitution stated that priests "must never leave their parishes unless they are constrained to do so for an important reason." If such a reason arose, before leaving he should entrust the sick and those women who were close to delivering a baby to the nearest parish priest.[52] Even when a legitimate reason existed to be absent from the parish, the constitutions made it clear that no member of the clergy may be absent from the diocese without having received a license from the archbishop or his vicar.[53] In order to ensure that priests follow the prescriptions of these decrees, Seripando exhorted the faithful to inform him or his vicar if their parish priest neglected to reside and carry out his obligation of service to those entrusted to his care.[54]

Since the eucharist was so essential for the spiritual well-being of the individual, Seripando ensured that the clergy celebrated Mass with due reverence. This was of great concern to him, for the synod issued twenty-two decrees dealing with the Mass. The clergy are reminded that they must celebrate the sacred mysteries with a sense of awe and reverence.[55] Seripando was also concerned that the clergy approach the eucharist with a proper disposition. Consequently, the synod ordered all priests not to approach the altar if their souls were not well-disposed and if they had not prepared their minds and hearts with study, diligence, and purity.[56]

Such a preparation involved an examination of conscience. The synod decreed that all priests prior to the celebration of the Mass should determine whether or not their conscience was stained with some sin. If they had sinned, they must suffer pain and grieve for their sins and be moved to repentance with tears of sadness. Once they had been cleansed they could appear before the presence of God.[57] To encourage this process, priests were ordered by the synodal constitutions to go to confession before celebrating the Mass because anyone who administered the blessed sacrament "must be cleansed not only before his own eyes . . . but more before the presence of God, which is done by contrition and in the eyes of the Church is done through confession."[58] Seripando went as far as to indicate that anyone who violated this prescription would be deprived of his license to celebrate the Mass.[59]

These decrees which emphasize the role of the clergy, along with the numerous prescriptions dealing with the actual celebration of the Mass, indicate the importance Seripando placed on the eucharist in the cultivation of the spiritual life and assisting the faithful toward their salvation.

For Seripando these decrees regulating the life of the clergy allowed them to carry out those works that rendered the Church holy, namely, to teach the doctrine of salvation, to administer the sacraments, to pray for the sins of the people and to offer the holy sacrifice.[60] By fulfilling these duties, and by reforming their lives so as to provide the faithful with examples of Christian living, the clergy fulfilled an essential role in Seripando's program of renewal for the diocese of Salerno.

### REFORM OF THE LAITY

There was a gap between the model of Christian living proposed by Seripando in his sermons and how people lived out their daily lives. The arrogance, avarice, violence, and so many other evils found among the people greatly troubled Seripando.

These practices had already been condemned by his predecessors, who through their vicars and pastoral visitations had a clear knowledge of the many examples of bad conduct among the laity, who engaged in numerous practices of questionable morality.[61] The situation had not really improved by the time Seripando assumed leadership of Salerno. Lamenting the influence of avarice in his day he underlined the fact that the people worshipped money as their god rather than Christ.[62]

Besides his concern with the manner in which the laity lived, Seripando was also concerned with the way in which the laity participated in the liturgical life of the Church. In his second sermon on the Lord's Prayer, he castigated the people for their demeanor during religious services. He began by stating that in the early Church the believers gathered to celebrate the mysteries of the faith with firmness and purity, unlike the practice in his own day. Seripando indicated that the Mass, the Divine Office, and the administration of the sacraments were all celebrated in the midst of disorder and confusion because the men and women gathered together not to pray but to converse with one another. These conversations, Seripando was certain, were unsuitable to Christian modesty. He also admonished the laity for the way they accompanied the eucharist to the home of the sick and dying. Rather than concerning themselves with the reality of death, their miseries, the grace which Christ brings to the infirm to whom this saving food of the soul was being brought, they occupied themselves with worldly concerns.[63] Seripando continued his admonition of the laity's conduct, observing that in the past it was unheard of to see people behave in such a manner that would give rise to laughter in holy places as he had seen in Salerno. He recalled the demeanor of some during the solemn vespers of Easter: they threw money with laughter, jokes, and profane conversation, as if they were engaged in children's games.[64] Seripando exhorted the faithful to abandon these bad and profane customs, to purge the holy places of such abuses, and to act like those who bear the name Christian.[65] The synodal constitutions also prohibited such behavior in the prescription that ordered the laity to do nothing more than pray when they were in church celebrating the Divine Office.[66]

Seripando reminded the laity of their duties as Christians as they assisted in fostering the holiness of the Church. He stated:

> The works of the faithful are to embody the doctrine of salvation, to partake of the sacraments, to participate in the prayers and Masses, to contemplate that which the ministers say and do . . . concerning the Sacred Mysteries, and to conform their minds and souls to what has been taught in word and deed by the ministers.[67]

By fulfilling these obligations the laity would be assisted in the cultivation of their spiritual life.

The development of the inner spiritual life of the laity was a primary concern for Seripando. This was the motivation behind the synodal constitutions that emphasized the teaching of doctrine and good customs ("*dottrina et buoni costumi*") to all the faithful, from the youngest to the oldest members of the congregation. Furthermore, models for the living out of the spiritual life should be presented to the faithful, especially the lives of the saints.[68] The obligation to teach the precepts of the spiritual life resided not only with the clergy, but also with parents and godparents.[69] The constitutions also emphasize the importance of the sacraments in the cultivation of the spiritual life. Thus, parents and godparents are to provide their children and godchildren with a good example by confessing and receiving communion regularly as a sign of their good faith in the sacraments.[70] In addition, the clergy should exhort the faithful each week of their need to confess regularly so that they will be worthy to receive Christ in the eucharist.[71]

With the penetration of unorthodox teachings into Italy, Seripando wanted to ensure that the laity were not contaminated by heretical ideas which threatened the unity of the Church. In his thirteenth sermon on the Lord's Prayer, he warned the faithful against false teaching:

> I say to you my children, be on guard against the ferment of the heretics, because they are still hypocrites and masters of lies. It is not a small thing to guard yourselves from them, because with hypocrisy they demonstrate sanctity, with lies they demonstrate a lofty doctrine, because they say things unheard of and which are not found in the other teachers and doctors of the truth.[72]

Seripando continued by exhorting the people not to believe these new teachings hastily or to abandon the faith of their ancestors easily, acknowledging that such a temptation existed because of the current state of the Church, which suffered from many abuses and problems. However, he reminded those leaning toward these new teachings to look at the fruits of these doctrines, which had given rise to various sects whose teachings contradicted each other.[73]

In order to prevent the spread of heresy in Salerno, the synodal constitutions prescribed that those harboring heretical ideas be made known to the archbishop. The constitution states:

> We order and command all those of whatever state of life or rank they may be, if they know or by chance come to know that someone is infected with Lutheran heresy, or any other heresy, or who speaks or has spoken badly of the sacraments and power of the Church, or of anything else pertaining to the Catholic faith, or who has books written by the heretics or those suspected of heresy, that they must, under the pain of incurring the sentence of excommunication, make them known to us within nine days of the publication of these our ordinances.[74]

Seripando was concerned about the penetration of these new teachings because of their disruptive nature to the unity of the Church, which represents for him the true sign of the mystical body. Those enemies of the Church who have disrupted its unity threaten, in Seripando's view, to extinguish the name of Christ in the world and destroy his Church. Thus, Seripando asks the faithful to pray each day that God will reunite into the body of the Church the alienated, the unfaithful, and the heretics, so that the unity of the mystical body will come to perfection and that Christ's promise of one flock with one shepherd, one body with one head, one bride with one bridegroom, will be realized in the Church.[75] Despite these concerns and prescriptions, it seems they were merely precautionary since Seripando indicates in his second sermon on the Apostles' Creed that as far as he was aware, there were no heretical beliefs circulating in Salerno at the time: "I find myself very happy, thanks be to God, because there has not come to my attention that among you there is another faith other than this one, nor even that there is any individual who reasons or says even one word against this faith."[76]

## REFORM OF FEMALE MONASTIC COMMUNITIES

Even prior to the Tridentine legislation, Seripando addressed the difficult task of reforming female monasteries, particularly in the area of observing monastic discipline and enclosure. The synod clearly ordered that nuns could not go outside of their monastery without having received a written license from the archbishop himself.[77] Not only were the nuns so prohibited, but others were forbidden from entering the monastery. The synod decreed that no men or women could enter a monastery, including doctors and confessors, even though their entrance might seem necessary, without the archbishop's written license, which would set strict time limitations on those who were given access to these monastic communities. Anyone who violated this prescription incurred the sentence of excommunication *ipso facto*.[78] Furthermore, any priest, besides the assigned chaplain, who entered a female monastic community to celebrate Mass without the license of the archbishop would be imprisoned for six months.[79]

In limiting contact between the nuns and the outside world, Seripando also restricted their conversation with others. The synod decreed that any conversation that took place between a nun and someone from the outside world, including family members, was to be done through a gate and in the presence of an older nun, who was to be chosen by the abbess at the time of the visitation.[80]

Since these female communities were to have little, if any, contact with the outside world, they had to provide for their needs and be able to support themselves without violating their vow of poverty. The synodal constitutions state that the abbess, along with two of the older nuns in the community chosen by the members, was to decide on the works engaged in by the community. While the constitutions do not spell out the kinds of works appropriate for female communities, they stipulate that these works must be honest and lawful.[81]

Because monastic enclosure was so important, several constitutions dealt with the means of assuring its observance. The constitutions stipulate that when the chaplain or confessor arrives in the church to prepare for the celebration of the sacraments, no nuns are to be present.[82] If any nuns enter the sacristy while the chaplain or confessor is there, they are to leave immediately without exchanging any words.[83] To preserve enclosure when the nuns spoke to visitors through iron grates, the constitutions dictated that the grates be so tightly woven together that the nun would hardly be visible or recognizable.[84] The same was to hold true in the confessional, where a heavy cloth was to be placed over the grate.[85] In terms of the windows within the monastery, including the windows in the church, they were to have blinds or shutters placed over them so that no one could be recognized or seen.[86] Finally, the nuns were not to receive any gifts or letters without the knowledge of the abbess, nor were they to send anyone gifts or letters without the permission of the abbess.[87] It was hoped that through these regulations, the female monastic communities would be restored to their original purity and renewed in the observance of their religious life.

## RESULTS OF THE SYNOD

Prior to the promulgation of the synodal decrees, Seripando wrote to Augusto Cocciano in Rome indicating that the clergy were receptive to the reforms: "I have already published a little bit of reform, which was moderate, so that it was voluntarily accepted by all, and as it seems to me it contains all the necessary items for the honest living of the clergy."[88] However, despite Seripando's positive assessment, the situation could not change instantaneously because the abuses had deep roots, making it difficult to implement his reform program. One year after the publication of the synodal decrees, he was forced to request a papal brief which would allow him to overcome certain difficulties with which he was faced, especially the claim of exemption from episcopal authority made by the various members of the clergy. On 30 January 1556, Paul IV issued the brief *Exigit tuae* to Seripando, which gave him the authority to visit, correct, and punish any person regardless of rank, including officials of the Roman Curia, laity or ecclesiastics directly or indirectly subject to the Holy See, and members of confraternities, any time they were guilty of some transgression.[89]

## PASTORAL VISITATION OF THE DIOCESE

With the authority received in *Exigit tuae*, Seripando could embark on the second stage of his reform program — the pastoral visitation of the diocese, which he hoped to begin personally a short time after the close of the synod. This would not be the first pastoral visitation undertaken in the diocese of Salerno. Between the years 1510-1553 the diocese, along with all its ecclesiastical institutions, was visited five times, approximately every seven years. Archbishop Federico Fregoso had ordered two pastoral visitations during his episcopacy, as did Archbishop Nicolo Ridolfi. Seripando's immediate predecessor, Ludovico de Torres, had also conducted a pastoral visitation.[90] Despite the frequency of these visitations, the bishops did not reside in the diocese, leaving its care and administration to vicars. While the vicars did their best to care for the diocese, they did not have sufficient authority to implement reform, contributing to the spiritual decline of the diocese.

Since Seripando believed that the reform of the clergy was a condition for the reform of the whole diocese, he thought it advisable to visit the diocese as a means of ensuring the implementation of the reforms promulgated by the synodal decrees and to gather information for any future regulations.[91] As one who took the obligation to reside seriously, he planned to make his way through the diocese, personally visiting the people, churches, and priests so as to listen to their desires and anxieties. In his letter of 24 October 1557 announcing the visitation, Seripando wrote that, given the great weight placed upon his shoulders for the care of their souls, from the outset of his episcopate he had "always proposed and desired to visit you personally and with our own eyes to see and to consider in every place the clergy and the people entrusted to us in order to console, exhort, admonish, and castigate anyone according to the needs which we would find."[92] However, poor health prohibited Seripando from carrying out the visitation personally. So as not to delay the visitation any longer, he entrusted this task to the bishop of Lesina, Orazio Greco:

> Not wanting, therefore, that our impediments bring harm to your salvation, nor seeming wise to delay any further this obligation of our office, we have decided to do through others that which the Lord God has not permitted us to do; for this reason, we send the Very Reverend Monsignor Bishop of Lesina, our vicar, to visit you according to the norms of the holy divine and human laws, to whom we have given and once again in this letter we give and confirm all of our power and authority to visit and to inquire principally into the things pertinent to the holy and Catholic faith and then to those things which touch upon the life and honesty of all our clergy and

finally all that is necessary for salvation and the Christian and spiritual life of all our people.[93]

Thus, Greco was charged with investigating the purity of doctrine, examining the conduct and morals of the clergy, and issuing regulations for the welfare of souls.

The visitation of the diocese began on 1 March 1557 in Solofra and continued uninterrupted until the twentieth of December of that same year. Beginning again in 1558, the visitations continued until June of that year. Seripando had written a letter which Greco was to read to the people at the beginning of each visit. In the letter Seripando explained his reason for not conducting the visitation personally and expresses the great pain he feels "of not being able personally to console you with God's word and to heal the wounds that you have received through the entrapments of the enemy of your salvation."[94]

From the pastoral visitation there emerged a positive picture of conditions in the diocese, suggesting that a rebirth of the spiritual and temporal life of the church in Salerno had begun. The churches were being repaired and were being better maintained.[95] Even the life of the clergy saw significant improvements. The register of priests for the years between 1555-1558 reveals that only thirty-one priests were at fault for transgressions. Of these, five were guilty of immorality and dishonest lives, while the remaining twenty-six were punished for being involved in brawls, usury, inflicting injuries on others, carrying arms, commercial fraud, homicide, and gambling. The pastoral visitation found approximately twenty members of the clergy who were ill prepared to carry out their ministry and ignorant of those things indispensable for the exercise of their priestly duties. Seripando's continual presence and vigilance, along with the reforms which he had prescribed in the synod and carried through with a paternal soul, but also with a firmness of decision, had altered the climate of the diocese, which was already experiencing a reform and renewal.

## OBSTACLES TO REFORM

As long as Seripando's reform efforts did not directly touch the cathedral chapter, he did not experience much opposition in the implementation of his program. Even when there was disagreement between himself and the chapter, he was able to surmount it and arrive at an agreeable solution. However, when Seripando's reform initiatives touched the cathedral chapter directly, his efforts to reorganize and discipline the customs of the chapter met stiff opposition. This resulted from the prominent social position which the members of the cathedral chapter held. Most of them came from noble families, and thus were jealous of their traditional privileges. Even with the receipt of a papal brief, Seripando was unable to overcome the challenge posed by the chapter in the area of reform.[96]

The cathedral chapter, composed of priests who were canons, was used to render the liturgical celebrations more solemn and to assist the bishop in the cathedral churches and to take his place during a vacancy. To understand the significance of Seripando's actions vis-à-vis the cathedral chapter, which he described as "contaminated by bad customs and by seditious persons who want neither order nor rules,"[97] it is necessary to consider briefly the general structure of this body and its functions and privileges.

The cathedral chapter can be understood as the senate of the diocese, whose functions vary according to the situations in which the diocese finds itself at a particular time. Often the bishop called upon the chapter to assist him in the spiritual and temporal administration of the diocese. During an episcopal vacancy, the cathedral chapter governed the diocese and elected the vicar general, who exercised most of the powers normally attributed to the bishop.[98] Clearly, the cathedral chapter played an important part in the spiritual life of the diocese and could influence the overall religious climate of the see. Given its prominence, it is not surprising that Seripando would want to reform this body and ensure that it would assist him in his reform initiatives.

After publishing the synodal decrees and executing the pastoral visitation of the diocese, Seripando turned his attention to reordering the duties of the cathedral chapter, in particular those things that dealt with liturgical worship and the administration of ecclesiastical property. He had dictated certain norms to control the choice of those eligible for the canonry and the functioning of certain offices. Thus, he stipulated that those candidates to be elected as canons had to be born of legitimate marriages; be of the proper age so that they could be ordained quickly if they were not already priests; be free of any grave vices, living according to good customs; be adequate in all those things demanded of the priestly status, especially in those things necessary for the worship and service of the Church; be educated and men of culture. Seripando also prescribed that the candidates always observe the synodal decree requiring the wearing of clerical garb and that those eligible had to have served in the Cathedral of Saint Matthew for at least two years, participating in the worship conducted in the cathedral and being present every Sunday and feast day in the choir at Mass and at vespers.[99]

In addition to issuing regulations prescribing the qualities that a candidate must possess and outlining the electoral process itself, Seripando also issued a series of norms which the canons, both those newly elected and those to be elected, were to observe. In the first place, the canon was obligated to observe all the synodal decrees. If the canon was in the habit of neglecting his service to the Church without a legitimate reason, he was to be deprived of his status and prebend. In an attempt to maintain stability within the chapter so that it could fulfill its functions Seripando ordered that any canon who engaged in activities that were prejudicial to the state of the chapter, its customs, its privileges, and other favors which the chapter possessed through the benignity of the Apostolic See, not only would be deprived of his canonry and prebend, but his entire family would be prohibited from attaining any ecclesiastical dignities within the cathedral church of Salerno.[100]

While the cathedral chapter accepted these provisions, their consent was merely formal and superficial. It would not be easy, after many years of neglect, to constrain the chapter under disciplinary norms. Yet Seripando, aware of the harmful consequences of the abuses within the cathedral chapter on the faithful, strove to initiate meaningful reform despite the opposition. It was necessary to assign the appropriate obligations and duties to the proper clerical rank within the chapter. Seripando also felt it necessary to regulate the authority of the masters of the friary, who were the true representatives of the chapter and the masters of the choir. Concerned with the administration of ecclesiastical property, Seripando proposed ways of better caring for and preserving the benefices attached to the prebends: the regulation of rents, rendering of accounts, and annual inspections of the land and buildings to assure proper maintenance of the properties.[101] In short, what Seripando hoped to do was to place both the internal and external life of the cathedral chapter upon a firm foundation. To accomplish this, he issued 177 articles, some gathered from earlier constitutions and others newly formulated.

Seripando's efforts led to tensions between the cathedral chapter and himself. Many felt that the new ordinances issued by the bishop undermined the rights and privileges of the chapter.[102] Given the resistance to the reforms, Seripando convoked the cathedral chapter on 19 October 1559 and through the intervention of Don Pietro Tolliero, auditor of the curia, insisted upon the acceptance of the reforms. Tolliero reminded the members of the chapter that Seripando had not only renewed the customs and ancient practices observed in the Church and by the clergy of Salerno, but he had issued new regulations as well for the good of his Church. Copies of these norms had been distributed among the members of the chapter for their careful consideration. Tolliero goes on to explain that he had been sent by Seripando to make the members of the chapter understand that the archbishop expected them to accept the reforms, which he issued for the benefit and peace of the church.[103] Despite Tolliero's efforts, the majority of the cathedral chapter resisted the reforms, in particular the masters of the friary, who, as arbitrators of the chapter, did not want to give up the liberty which they had always enjoyed.

The dispute between the chapter and Seripando remained at an impasse, prompting him to seek the intervention of the newly elected pope, Pius IV. The pope had his Master of the Sacred Palace examine the new constitutions issued by Seripando. In 1560 Pius IV issued a brief, *Cum sicut accepimus*, approving eighty-nine of the most important constitutions and giving Seripando the right to control sacred rites on the minor feast days of the year.[104] In the meantime, the chapter had chosen a group of representatives to continue discussions with the archbishop. Realizing the gravity of the situation, the canon Mattia Borda implored the newly chosen representatives not to bring ruin to the Church but to enter these discussions with the aim of giving honor to God, dignity to the church, and service to the archbishop.[105]

On 8 April 1561, the vicar general of Salerno, Girolamo Sciabica, convened the cathedral chapter in Seripando's absence, because he had already left for the Council of Trent, and presented its members with the papal brief issued by Pius IV, believing this would finally bring an end to the dispute. However, this was not to be. The new constitutions were read aloud word for word, without any open opposition on the part of the canons. In fact, some accepted the constitutions openly, while others requested that they be given copies so as to be able to carefully read and consider the constitutions before accepting them. This was done, but rather than accept the constitutions, the chapter formed a delegation to appeal them before Pius IV.[106] However, one month later the chapter dropped its appeal, perhaps realizing the futility of seeking an appeal of a papal brief. In a meeting of the cathedral chapter held on 7 May 1561, the members of the chapter accepted the reform constitutions, merely seeking some clarifications of certain provisions from Seripando, whom they characterized as their "benign pastor and father." The chapter goes on to indicate that they found nothing prejudicial to the rights and privileges of the chapter in the constitutions, but rather holy, just, and useful things for the benefit of the Church. In addition, they found many things which favored the chapter and were grateful to Seripando for issuing these constitutions.[107]

While a change had taken place within the chapter, it did not cease to seek clarifications of the various reform constitutions. In fact, on the day Seripando died in Trent, the cathedral chapter met in Salerno to discuss once again the constitutions that had been approved by Pius IV. With Seripando's death, the four-year controversy with the cathedral chapter came to an end, as did the constitutions themselves. When Seripando's successor Gaspare Cervantes inquired of a canon during a pastoral visitation about the constitutions that had been issued by Seripando, he responded, "the constitutions were lost during the period of the vacancy,"[108] illustrating the chapter's resistance to reform.

The cathedral chapter was not the only group within the diocese that opposed Seripando's program for religious reform. Since his first attempts at reform upon his arrival in Salerno, the exempt religious had tried to resist his initiatives. To assist him in overcoming these difficulties, Pius IV issued a *motu proprio* on 27 March 1560 for the purpose of visiting and reforming exempt religious, which gave Seripando all those powers that had been given to reforming bishops since the pontificate of Paul III.

> Among these powers was the important provision that the visitator had the right to suspend or remove incompetent parish priests and to make new appointments by papal authority. Seripando was further given authority to visit and reform those in-

corporated parishes belonging to monks living in monasteries and to appoint competent priests for the care of souls in such parishes at the cost of the religious beneficiary.[109]

It was somewhat ironic that Seripando sought such authority, given the fact that during the first period of the Council of Trent he had been the principal defender of the freedoms and prerogatives of religious preachers from the control of local bishops. This apparent inconsistency in his outlook can be understood in light of the fact that it was essential for him to receive this authority over the exempt religious within his diocese if he was to accomplish his reform agenda.

Pius IV's appointment of Girolamo Seripando as a legate to the Council of Trent forced him, after six years of continual residency, to be absent from his diocese. Indeed, Seripando would never again return to his diocese, dying at Trent while serving as a conciliar legate. Yet, despite his absence and his many responsibilities as legate, he did not lose sight of his diocese. He tried his best to guide the diocese in the spirit of the reforms he had initiated, even from afar. Before leaving for Rome, and then Trent, he entrusted the administration of the diocese to his nephew, Marcello Seripando, the vicar general, Girolamo Sciabica, and the auditor, Francesco Longo.[110]

Remaining in regular contact with these individuals, Seripando realized that things were not running smoothly in Salerno. He wrote to the vicar general complaining about the way he was administering the diocese and threatening to take measures to rectify the situation. Seripando indicated to Sciabica that despite his many responsibilities at Trent, he remained concerned about the situation in Salerno. He desired that Sciabica continue the reform efforts that he had begun in the diocese.[111] Desiring to keep on top of the circumstances in his diocese, Seripando wrote to Sciabica on 15 September 1561 that he should inform him as often as necessary about circumstances and problems in Salerno because he had not forgotten Salerno and wished to know about the affairs in the diocese.[112]

That he was worried about the state of Salerno despite his responsibilities as a legate is also evident in his letters to his nephew Marcello. Aware of the problems he was having with the cathedral chapter and exempt orders while he was in residence, he was disturbed by the news he was receiving from Salerno. He wrote to his nephew, "Of the things of Salerno I do not have hope that they can go well, because if this was not the case when I was present, how could it be now that I am absent?"¹¹³ His worry became distressful torment, and he sought to offer some remedies, exhorting, warning, and repeating clear and precise directives to those he left in charge. He writes to Marcello, "The things of Salerno give me every day more torment of the soul. I will not stop, however, providing remedies as much as I am able to."¹¹⁴ Thus, despite the fact that he was not physically present in his diocese, Seripando continued to govern and guide his diocese personally even from afar. This period reveals his sincerity as a reformer and the continuity with his views on residency and the role and responsibility of the bishop.

## CONCLUSION

The element that characterized the pastoral work of Girolamo Seripando aside from the synod, the pastoral visitation, and the various reform decrees was his constant presence among the people. He especially made his presence felt among the youth of Salerno, upon whom he hoped to promote the good of the Church and of the city. Furthermore, he applied himself to the reestablishment of the confraternities, which were dedicated to the rediscovery of piety and popular spirituality.¹¹⁵

In all of these ways, Seripando's episcopacy marked the beginning of Catholic reform in Salerno. In his brief reign as bishop, Seripando attempted to correct the abuses he found in the diocese when he arrived in 1554 with a guiding sternness that tolerated no transgressions. While the prescriptions codified in the synodal decrees set in motion a reform and renewal of the diocese, he was unable to eradicate all the abuses and problems that afflicted the spiritual life of Salerno. He himself attests so often in his sermons to the failure to alter the way of life and habits of the clergy and the faithful, evidencing how deeply rooted the abuses had become. In his first sermon on the Apostles' Creed Seripando observes: "I have noticed during the past two years that those discourses I delivered, which were born of a paternal love, have not been fruitful, because I have not seen you become, my dearest children, more wise, more just, more holy, or more free. In fact, it seems to me that in each of these areas you have become worse."¹¹⁶ A similar picture is painted by Seripando in his seventh sermon on the Lord's Prayer when he warns, "I want to pull your ears and awaken you from the serious sleep in which I see you buried."[117] In the same sermon, he states, "You deserve a good chastisement for allowing the gospel to fall into the dirt . . . among the dogs and pigs."[118]

Yet, despite the limited effects of Seripando's reform program and the greater attention often paid to the reform efforts of his successors, one circumstance places Seripando's work in a more favorable light. It was his episcopacy that laid the foundations for reform. Seripando made the difficult beginning, encountering many obstacles with which his successors did not have to contend. Furthermore, the bishops who came after him could rest on the reform decrees of the Council of Trent, which had been confirmed by Pius IV and provided them with a clear set of norms by which they could guide their own efforts.[119] Girolamo Seripando came to Salerno and found a church in need of religious renewal. Armed with his understanding of the role and function of the bishop, he set out immediately to restore the clergy and the faithful by initiating a reform that reflected the spirit of the early Church. It was through his efforts that the church of Salerno was pushed in a new direction. Seripando's episcopacy marks a vigorous reawakening of souls and the beginning of a renewal that changed every facet of the spiritual and religious life in the diocese of Salerno. When Seripando left Salerno, the spiritual terrain of the diocese had been altered, and the clergy and the people were prepared to accept the Tridentine reforms.

## NOTES

1. Larissa Taylor, *Soldiers of Christ: Preaching in Late Medieval and Reformation France* (New York: Oxford University Press, 1992), 121.

2. Girolamo Seripando, "Prediche Salernitane," in Rocchina M. Abbondanza, *Girolamo Seripando tra Evangelismo e Riforma Cattolica* (Naples: Ferraro, 1982), 87ff.

3. PRS, 87.

4. Alessandro Fava, "La restaurazione cattolica nella Diocesi di Salerno—L'Arcivescovo Seripando," *Rassegna Storica Salernitana* 1 (1938): 106.

5. Antonio Balducci, *Girolamo Seripando: Arcivescovo di Salerno, 1554-1563* (Cava dei Tirreni: Arti Grafiche di Mauro, 1963), 21-22.

6. Ibid., 24.

7. Ibid., 25-26.

8. See Chapter two.

9. BNN, MSS COD XIII, AA, vol. 61, f. 115.

10. BNN, MSS COD XIII, AA, vol. 54, f. 15.
11. Donato Dente, *Salerno nel Seicento: Nell'Interno di una città*, vol. 1: *Istituzioni culturali* (Salerno: Edisud, 1990), 211.
12. Ibid. See also Abbondanza, 25.
13. Donato Dente, *Salerno nel Seicento: Nell'Interno di una città*, vol. 2, pt. 1: *Inediti per la Storia Civile e Religiosa* (Salerno: Edisud, 1993), 292.
14. Abbondanza, 25.
15. Ibid.
16. Balducci, 55.
17. Julius III, *Magnitudo meritorum*, BAV, R.G. Concili IV, 222 (1).
18. BNN, MSS COD XIII, AA, vol. 61, f. 115.
19. BNN, Vind. Lat. 64, f. 17r.
20. Ibid.
21. Ibid.
22. Generoso Crisci, *Il cammino della Chiesa Salernitana nell'opera dei suoi Vescovi*, 4 vols. (Naples: Libreria Editrice Redenzione, 1976-1984), 1: 537.
23. "Costituzioni Sinodali," in *Memorie per servire alla storia della Chiesa Salernitana*, 4 vols., ed. Giuseppe Paesano (Salerno: Raffaello Migliaccio, 1846-1857), 4: 390.
24. Ibid., 4: 390-91.
25. Dente, *Inediti per la Storia*, 327.
26. Ibid. See also Balducci, 23.
27. PS, 281.
28. Ibid., 283.
29. BNN, MSS COD XIII, AA, vol. 61, f. 127.
30. Ernesto Pontieri, "La cultura umanistico-rinascimentale in Italia e la Chiesa Cattolica," in *Divagazioni Storiche e Storiografiche*, 2a seria (Naples: Libreria Scientifica, 1971), 294.
31. Balducci, 28.
32. Ibid., 29.
33. Ibid.
34. CS VI, "Della Confessione, et delli Confessori," 4: 406.
35. Ibid.
36. CS I, "Ordinatione," 4: 407.
37. CS II, "Ordinatione," 4: 407.
38. CS III, "Ordinatione," 4: 407.
39. CS III, "Della Confessione, et delli Confessori," 4: 405.
40. CS IV, "Della Confessione, et delli Confessori," 4: 405.
41. CS III, "Della Confessione, et delli Confessori," 4: 405.
42. Balducci, 63.
43. PRS, 212.
44. CS I, "Delli Curati et Ministri delli Sacramenti," 4: 413.
45. Abbondanza, 32.

46. CS III, "Delli Curati et Ministri delli Sacramenti," 4: 413.
47. Abbondanza, 72.
48. CS I, "L'honestà della vita," 4: 409-10.
49. CS IV, "L'honestà della Vita," 4: 410-11.
50. CS IV, VI, VII, "L'honestà della Vita," 4: 410-12.
51. Abbondanza, 31-2.
52. CS IX, "Delli Curati et Ministri delli Sacramenti," 4: 414-15.
53. CS X, "Delli Curati et Ministri delli Sacramenti," 4: 415.
54. CS IX, "Delli Curati et Ministri delli Sacramenti," 4: 414-15.
55. CS II, "Del Sacrificio della Messa," 4: 398.
56. CS VII, "Del Sacrificio della Messa," 4: 399.
57. CS IX, "Del Sacrificio della Messa," 4: 399-400.
58. CS X, "Del Sacrificio della Messa," 4: 400.
59. Ibid.
60. PS, 282.
61. Dente, *Inediti per la Storia*, 298.
62. Ibid., 299.
63. PRS, 97.
64. Ibid., 97-98.
65. Ibid., 97.
66. CS I, "I Laici," 4: 428.
67. PS, 283.
68. CS XV, "Delli Curati et Ministri delli Sacramenti," 4: 416.
69. CS XVI, "Delli Curati et Ministri delli Sacramenti," 4: 416.
70. Ibid.
71. CS VII, "Delli Curati et Ministri delli Sacramenti," 4: 414.
72. PRS, 222.
73. Ibid.
74. CS, "Heretici," 4: 422-23.
75. PRS, 237.
76. PS, 66.
77. CS I, "Le Monache," 4: 423.
78. CS II, "Le Monache," 4: 423.
79. CS IV, "Le Monache," 4: 424.
80. CS III, "Le Monache," 4: 423.
81. CS VII, "Le Monache," 4: 424.
82. CS IX, "Le Monache," 4: 424.
83. CS X, "Le Monache," 4: 425.
84. CS XII, "Le Monache," 4: 425.
85. CS XIV, "Le Monache," 4: 425.
86. CS XVI, "Le Monache," 4: 425-26.
87. CS XVII, "Le Monache," 4: 426.
88. BNN, MSS COD XIII, AA, vol. 61, f. 125.
89. Paul IV, *Exigit tuae*, BAV, R.G. Concili IV, 222 (1).
90. Balducci, 18.

91. Hubert Jedin, *Papal Legate at the Council of Trent, Cardinal Seripando*, trans. Frederic C. Eckhoff (St. Louis: B. Herder Book Co., 1947), 476.
92. *Lettera per la visita pastorale*, in Balducci, 91.
93. Ibid.
94. Ibid.
95. Balducci, 68.
96. Abbondanza, 34.
97. Dente, *Inediti per la Storia*, 337.
98. Ibid., 338.
99. Balducci, 95-96.
100. Ibid., 97.
101. Ibid., 74.
102. *Sessione Capitolare del 21 agosto 1559 con intervento del Sindaco ed Eletto per le consuetudini et riti*, in Balducci, 107.
103. *Sessione capitolare del 19 ottobre 1559*, in Balducci, 108.
104. Balducci, 75.
105. Ibid., 76.
106. Ibid.
107. Ibid., 79.
108. Ibid., 80.
109. Jedin, *Papal Legate*, 480.
110. Fava, 121.
111. "Letter of Seripando to the Vicar, Abbot Sciabica (14 August 1561)," in Hubert Jedin, *Girolamo Seripando Sein Leben und Denken in Geisteskampf des 16 Jahrhunderts* (Würzburg: Rita Verlag, 1937), 634.
112. BNN, MSS COD XIII, AA, vol. 58, f. 21.
113. Crisci, 1: 552.
114. Ibid.
115. Donato Dente, "Vita culturale ed istituzioni scolastiche a Salerno nel Cinquecento: Note e Documenti," in *Salerno e il Principato Citra nell'età moderna (secoli XVI-XIX)*, ed. Francesco Sofia (Naples: Edizioni Scientifiche Italiane, 1987), 843.
116. PS, 42.
117. PRS, 152.
118. PRS, 149.
119. Jedin, *Papal Legate*, 487.

## CHAPTER SIX

# CONCLUSION

The Catholic reformers of the sixteenth century placed all their hopes for the renewal and regeneration of the Church on a restored episcopacy. Looking back to the bishops of antiquity, who were present to their people as preachers and shepherds, it was evident that this image had been tarnished as bishops neglected their duties and obligations. The more the bishops of the sixteenth century neglected their ecclesiastical responsibilities, the more the reform movement pointed out the discrepancy between the ideal and the actual condition of the hierarchy. While the Council of Trent would issue reform legislation that would ultimately alter the state of the episcopacy, a handful of bishops had already begun to reform the episcopal office, serving as models for the discussions later held at Trent. As this study has demonstrated, Girolamo Seripando must be counted among this group of bishops.

There is no doubt among historians that Girolamo Seripando was one of the leading personalities of pre-Tridentine reform. Because of his humanist background and his relations with the major proponents of the various lay and religious intellectual currents of that era, he has often been portrayed as a leading theologian and effective reformer of the Augustinian Order, of which he was a member. Much attention, too, has been given to the important contributions he made to the deliberations at Trent, particularly in his capacity as legate. While he achieved a great degree of success in each of these areas, it seems that his truly pioneering work as a reformer came during his brief rule as archbishop of Salerno. The character and tone of Seripando's episcopacy prepared the way for the Tridentine-type bishop that would emerge in the post-conciliar period.

Unlike the vast majority of the bishops of his day, Seripando rested his entire reform program on residency. He believed that any truly meaningful reform could be initiated only if the bishop was personally present among his people, aware of their spiritual and religious concerns and needs. By residing in the diocese, he was able to fulfill his primary function as a bishop, namely to preach. The themes expressed in Seripando's sermons reflect not only his own spiritual life and thought, but also the Augustinian tradition from which he emerges. For Seripando, the help of souls was the principal aim of his preaching. Consequently, his sermons bear witness to a proponent of the renewal of religious and spiritual life based upon moral and religious values whose roots are found in scripture, particularly Saint Paul, and the Church Fathers, most especially the spiritual teachings of Augustine. Whether he addressed his sermons to the laity, the clergy, or members of his own religious order, they resulted from his own reflections on the truths of the faith, the spiritual tradition of the Augustinians, and his own spirituality. Based on scriptural and patristic themes and his own personal devotion, Seripando's sermons spoke to the practical spiritual needs of his listeners. He hoped and desired to move the listener to lead a better Christian life.

The sermons of Girolamo Seripando, then, developed a theology aimed at the *cura animarum*, the religious instruction of the people, and the faithful living out of the Christian message. His ability to fuse theological teaching with the spiritual and material needs of the people of Salerno gave his sermons a specific character. By tailoring each sermon to the various groups present within the congregation, his sermons were instruments by which he could correct the customs and way of life of his flock, along with the teaching of doctrine. In this way, the sermons formed an integral part of Seripando's vast program to reform the diocese of Salerno.

The reform program Seripando hoped to put in place corresponded with those movements within the Church that worked toward the moral, intellectual, and spiritual reform and renewal of the institution and its members. This reform initiative reflected the spirituality of the humanists of his day, who hoped to restore the *ecclesia primitiva*, which they perceived as a spiritual Church that was simple and holy. They believed that if the Church was to experience a regeneration it was necessary to return to the spirit of the gospel which animated the ecclesiastical communities of the apostolic and patristic eras.

Seripando's success rested on just such a restoration. Within his own person he restored the image of the bishop found in the epistles of Saint Paul and the homilies and letters of the bishops of the patristic age. Thus, with Seripando, the bishop as preacher, teacher, and pastor of souls was once again at the heart of the Christian community. For him, the personal presence and governance of the diocese by the bishop was the foundation for all pastoral reform. By reviving the patristic image of the bishop, Girolamo Seripando not only represents one of the earliest of the Tridentine-type bishops, but also a bishop who was able to introduce norms that initiated a process of renewal of the spiritual life of the church in Salerno, prior to being legislated by the Council of Trent.

Given the similarity between the reform decrees issued by the Council of Trent regarding the office of bishop and Seripando's own reform program in Salerno, one may conclude that his own experience as a bishop had an impact on the conciliar discussions. The Council of Trent decreed that bishops must reside in their diocese;[1] summon synods on a regular basis;[2] make visitations of their diocese;[3] preach regularly;[4] explain the power and benefit of the sacraments to the faithful, along with the divine commandments and precepts of salvation;[5] correct abuses among the clergy and the laity;[6] watch over the female religious communities;[7] ordain only suitable candidates;[8] and provide for the religious instruction of the children in his diocese.[9] Each of these prescriptions had been part of Seripando's episcopacy from the outset. It can, therefore, be argued that Seripando not only embodied the Catholic Reformation's image of the bishop, but helped to shape the image of the Tridentine bishop that would become the model in the decades after the Council.

Girolamo Seripando will certainly remain one of the most illustrious of Salerno's archbishops. His significance comes from his ability to implement a series of reforms which allowed for the spiritual renewal of Salerno through the cultivation of the inner spiritual life founded upon participation in the sacramental life of the Church, most especially the eucharist; the formation and improvement of the life of the clergy; the religious and moral education of the faithful. This reform program did not repudiate traditional dogma, the liturgy, the hierarchy, or ecclesiastical unity. Rather it was a response to the spiritual needs of an age that yearned for a more vibrant faith and a religious expression and spirituality that reflected the experience of people in their daily activities.

The brief episcopate of Girolamo Seripando provides a picture of what the reformers of the sixteenth century envisioned as a model of the restored episcopacy. His episcopate can no longer be overshadowed by his many other accomplishments as prior general of the Augustinian Order or legate at the Council of Trent, but must be acknowledged as a significant phase in the efforts to restore the Church to its former pristine state. His efforts in this area made him a proponent of Catholic reform, that is, the renewal of the spiritual and religious life of Catholicism based on the gospels, the ideals of the primitive apostolic Church, and the teachings of the Church Fathers, particularly, for Seripando, Saint Augustine. Through his pastoral reform program, reflected in the prescriptions of the synodal constitutions and the themes expressed in his sermons, Seripando reanimated the spiritual life of Salerno.

It is as archbishop of Salerno that Girolamo Seripando can be ranked among those few pioneering reformers, such as Gian Matteo Giberti, bishop of Verona, who viewed episcopal reform as the very essence of the Catholic Reformation. The episcopacies of Charles Borromeo in Milan and Gabriele Paleotti in Bologna are often heralded as the great models of Tridentine reform. It is time to place Girolamo Seripando among these outstanding bishops as one who prefigured and paved the way for the Tridentine model.

## NOTES

1. *Decree on Reform*, Session 23, canon 1 in Norman P. Tanner, *Decrees of the Ecumenical Councils*, 2 vols. (Washington, DC: Georgetown University Press, 1990), 2: 744. Subsequent references to the conciliar decrees will come from this collection.
2. *Decree on Reform*, Session 24, canon 2, 2:761.
3. *Decree on Reform*, Session 24, canon 3, 2:761.
4. *Decree on Reform*, Session 24, canon 4, 2:763.
5. *Decree on Reform*, Session 24, canon 7, 2:764.
6. *Decree on Reform*, Session 24, canon 10, 2:765.
7. *Decree on Reform*, Session 25, canon 10, 2:779.
8. *Decree on Reform*, Session 23, canon 7, 2:747.
9. *Decree on Reform*, Session 24, canon 4, 2:763.

# A SELECTED BIBLIOGRAPHY

I. PRIMARY SOURCES

MANUSCRIPT SOURCES

Biblioteca Apostolica Vaticana, Rome

*Vat. Lat. 6189.* Lettere di Girolamo Seripando a Guglielmo Sirleto.

*Vat. Lat. 6692.* Lettere di Girolamo Seripando al Cardinale Carlo Borromeo circa le cose del Concilio di Trento.

*Vat. Lat. 6694.* Lettere di Girolamo Seripando a diversi.

Biblioteca Nazionale Vittorio Emmanuele III, Naples

MSS COD VIII, AA, vol. 22.

*Mystica cena Christianorum.*

*Lettere di Girolamo Seripando.*

MSS COD VIII, AA, vol. 26.

*De episcoporum duplici generat eorum officio.*

*De multis in civitate necessariis Episcopis.*

*Ingressus ad Episcopatum.*

*Episcopatus hoc tempore cur fugiendus.*

*Episcopi descriptio ex Pauli doctrina.*

*De episcoporum max. pondere.*

*De episcoporum gravi certamine.*

*De episcoporum summo periculo.*

*De episcoporum principali officio defensione et tutela veritatis.*

*De modo recipiendi Christum tanque sapientiam.*

*De modo recipiendi Christum tanque iustitiam.*

*De modo recipiendi Christum tanque sanctificatione.*

*De modo recipiendi Christum tanque redemptionem.*

*De Eucharistia Sacro ex Verbis Dni.*

*De Ps. XLVIII.*

*In memoria subsidium.*

MSS COD XIII, AA, vol. 48.

*Lettere di Girolamo Seripando.*

MSS COD XIII, AA, vol. 50.

*Lettere di Augusto Cocciano a Girolamo Seripando.*

*Lettere di Girolamo Seripando a Augusto Cocciano.*

MSS COD XIII, AA, vol. 54.

*Descrizione della diocesi di Salerno scritta dall'arcivescovo Girolamo Seripando.*

MSS COD XIII, AA, vol. 55.

*Lettere di Girolamo Seripando.*

MSS COD XIII, AA, vol. 58.

*Lettere di Girolamo Seripando.*

MSS COD XIII, AA, vol. 61.

*Lettere di Girolamo Seripando a Augusto Cocciano e la risposta di Cocciano.*

Vind. Lat. 64.

*Lettera di Girolamo Seripando all'imperatore Carlo V.*

*Breve di Papa Giulio III a Seripando (26 aprile 1554).*

Biblioteca Statale Angelica, Rome

MSS 762. *Card. Hieronymi Seripandi, ad eumdem Jo. Fr. epistolae 5 italicae, dd. Tridenti.*

MSS 780. *De septima petitione orationis Dominice.*

# PRINTED SOURCES

Algranati, Gina. *Saggio di una biografia del Cardinale Seripando*. Foggia: Leone, 1911.

Balducci, Antonio. *Girolamo Seripando: Arcivescovo di Salerno, 1554-1563*. Cava dei Tirreni: Arti Grafiche di Mauro, 1963.

*Concilium Tridentinum. Diariorum, actorum, epistolarum, tractatum nova collectio*. 13 vols. Ed. Societas Goerresiana. Freiburg: Herder, 1901-1938.

Crisci, Generoso. *Il cammino della chiesa salernitana nell'opera dei suoi vescovi*. 4 vols. Naples: Libreria Editrice Redenzione, 1976-1984.

Gutiérrez, David. "Hieronymi Seripandi 'Diarium de Vita Sua' (1513-1562)." *Analecta Augustiniana* 26 (1963): 5-193.

_____. "Ex Hieronymi Seripandi 'Diario' Folium Primum Ineditum." *Analecta Augustiniana* 27 (1964): 334-340.

Jedin, Hubert. *Girolamo Seripando Sein Leben und Denken im Geisteskampf des 16 Jahrhunderts*. Wurzburg: Rita Verlag, 1937.

Julius III. *Magnitudo meritorum*. Biblioteca Apostolica Vaticana. R.G. Concili, IV, 222 (1).

Marranzini, Alfredo. *Dibattito Lutero Seripando su "Giustizia e Libertà del Cristiano."* Brescia: Morcelliana, 1981.

Martène, E. and Durand, U. *Veterum scriptorum et monumentorum ecclesiasticorum et dogmaticorum amplissima collectio*. 9 vols. Paris, 1724-1733.

Olin, John C. *The Catholic Reformation: Savonarola to Ignatius Loyola*. Westminster, MD: Christian Classics, Inc., 1969.

Paesano, Giuseppe. *Memorie per servire alla storia della chiesa salernitana*. 4 vols. Salerno: Raffaello Migliaccio, 1846-1847.

Patavinus, Christophorus. *Canones Verbi Dei Concionatoribus Ordinis Fratrum Eremitarum S. Augustini*. Rome, 1555.

Paul IV. *Exigit tuae*. Biblioteca Apostolica Vaticana. R.G. Concili IV, 222 (1).

Seripando, Girolamo. *Doctrina Orandi, sive expositio orationis dominica*. Louvain: Bernardini Masij, 1661.

_____. *Prediche di Girolamo Seripando Arcivescovo di Salerno*. Ed. Francesco Linguiti. Salerno: Raffaello Migliaccio, 1858.

_____. "Vita del Cardinale Girolamo Seripando uno dei legati del Concilio di Trento scritto a modo di Giornale da lui medesimo." *Docu-*

menti inediti e nuovi lavori letterarii sul Concilio di Trento. Ed. Generoso Calenzio. Rome: Sinimberghi, 1874.

---------. "Prediche Salernitane." *Girolamo Seripando tra Evangelismo e Riforma Cattolica*. Rocchina M. Abbondanza. Naples: Ferraro, 1982.

Tanner, Norman P. Ed. *Decrees of the Ecumenical Councils*. 2 vols. Washington, DC: Georgetown University Press, 1990.

## II. SECONDARY SOURCES

Abbondanza, Rocchina M. *Girolamo Seripando tra Evangelismo e Riforma Cattolica*. Naples: Ferraro, 1982.

Algranati, Gina. *Vita di Fra Geronimo Seripando*. Naples: Francesco Perella, 1923.

Aumann, Jordan. *Christian Spirituality in the Catholic Tradition*. San Francisco: Ignatius Press, 1985.

Balducci, Antonio. *Girolamo Seripando: Arcivescovo di Salerno, 1554-1563*. Cava dei Tirreni: Arti Grafiche di Mauro, 1963.

Bornstein, Daniel E. *The Bianchi of 1399: Popular Devotion in Late Medieval Italy*. Ithica: Cornell University Press, 1993.

Bouwsma, William J. "The Spirituality of Renaissance Humanism." *Christian Spirituality: High Middle Ages and Reformation*. Ed. Jill Raitt. New York: Crossroad, 1987.

Caponetto, Salvatore. *La riforma protestante nell'Italia del Cinquecento*. Torino: Claudiana, 1992.

Cesareo, Francesco C. "Penitential Sermons in Renaissance Italy: Girolamo Seripando and the Pater Noster." *The Catholic Historical Review* 83 (1997): 1-19.

---------. "Reflections of a Shepherd: The Sermons of Girolamo Seripando." *Augustinian Heritage* 39 (1993): 177-189.

---------. "Patristic and Humanist Themes in the Sermons of Girolamo Seripando." *Analecta Augustiniana* 56 (1993): 265-278.

---------. "Humanist Spirituality and Religious Reform in Salerno: The Case of Girolamo Seripando." *Augustinian Heritage* 38 (1992): 189-201.

---------. "The Image of Bishop in the Sermons of Girolamo Seripando." *Augustinian Heritage* (1992): 7-21.

Chacon, Alfonso. *Vitae et res gestae Pontificium Romanorum et S.R.E. Cardinalium*. 4 vols. Rome, 1677.

Ciolini, Gino. "Scrittori spirituali Agostiniani dei secoli XIV e XV in Italia." *Sanctus Augustinus Vitae Spiritualis Magister*. Rome: Analecta Augustiniana, 1959.

Cosimato, Donato. *Salerno nel Seicento: Economia e società*. Salerno: Laveglia, 1989.

Crisci, Generoso and Campagna, Angelo. *Salerno Sacra: Ricerche Storiche*. Salerno: Edizioni della Chiesa Arcivescovile, 1962.

D'Amico, John F. *Renaissance Humanism in Papal Rome: Humanists and Churchmen on the Eve of the Reformation*. Baltimore: The Johns Hopkins University Press, 1983.

Del Grosso, Maria Antonietta. *Salerno nel Seicento: Nell'Interno di una città. Vol. 2, pt. 2: Le Attività Economiche*. Salerno: Edisud, 1993.

Dente, Donato. *Salerno nel Seicento: Nell'Interno di una città. Vol. 2, pt. 1: Inediti per la Storia Civile e Religiosa*. Salerno: Edisud, 1993.

_____. *Salerno nel Seicento: Nell'Interno di una città. Vol. 1: Istituzioni Culturali*. Salerno: Edisud, 1990.

_____. "Vita culturale ed istituzioni scolastiche a Salerno nel Cinquecento: Note e Documenti." *Salerno e il Principato Citra nell'età moderna (secoli XVI-XIX)*. Ed. Francesco Sofia. Naples: Edizioni Scientifiche Italiane, 1987.

Evennett, H. Outram. *The Spirit of the Counter Reformation*. Cambridge: Cambridge University Press, 1968.

Fava, Alessandro. "La restaurazione cattolica nella Diocesi di Salerno — L'arcivescovo Seripando." *Rassegna Storica Salernitana* 1 (1938): 105-123.

Firpo, Massimo. *Riforma protestante ed eresie nell'Italia del Cinquecento*. Rome: Laterza, 1993.

Gindle, Egon. *Bibliografie zur Geschichte und Theologie des Augustiner-Eremitenordens bis zum beginn der Reformation*. Berlin: De Gruyter, 1977.

Gleason, Elisabeth G. *Gasparo Contarini: Venice, Rome, and Reform*. Berkeley: University of California Press, 1993.

Grendler, Paul F. *Schooling in Renaissance Italy: Literacy and Learning, 1300-1600*. Baltimore: The Johns Hopkins University Press, 1989.

Gutiérrez, David. *The Augustinians from the Protestant Reformation to the Peace of Westphalia, 1518-1648*. Villanova: Augustinian Historical Institute, 1979.

_____. *Los Agustinos desde el protestantismo hasta la restauración católica, 1518-1648*. Rome: Institutum Historicum Ordinis Fratrum S. Augustini, 1971.

_____. "Seripando, teólogo y legado en el Concilio de Trento." *La Ciudad de Dios* 178 (1965): 62-104.

_____. "Españoles del siglo XVI en el epistolario de Seripando." *La Ciudad de Dios* 178 (1964): 234-266.

_____. "Hieronymi Seripandi Scripta." *Latinitatis* 12 (April 1964): 142-152.

Headley, John M. and Tomaro, John B. Eds. *San Carlo Borromeo: Catholic Reform and Ecclesiastical Politics in the Second Half of the Sixteenth Century.* Washington, DC: The Folger Shakespeare Library, 1988.

Hudon, William V. *Marcello Cervini and Ecclesiastical Government in Tridentine Italy.* DeKalb: Northern Illinois University Press, 1992.

Jedin, Hubert. *Papal Legate at the Council of Trent, Cardinal Seripando.* Trans. Frederic C. Eckhoff. St. Louis: B. Herder Book Co., 1947.

_____. *A History of the Council of Trent.* Vols. 1-2. Translated by Ernest Graf. St. Louis: B. Herder Book Co., 1949.

_____. "Seelenleitung und Vollkommenheitsstreben bei Kardinal Seripando." *Sanctus Augustinus Vitae Spiritualis Magister.* Rome: Analecta Augustiniana, 1959.

_____. and Dolan, John, eds. *History of the Church.* Vol. 5, *Reformation and Counter Reformation*, by Erwin Iserloh, Joseph Glazik, and Hubert Jedin. New York: The Seabury Press, 1980.

Kristeller, Paul O. *Renaissance Thought and Its Sources.* Ed. Michael Mooney. New York: Columbia University Press, 1979.

_____. *Medieval Aspects of Renaissance Learning.* Durham: Duke University Press, 1974.

Linguiti, Francesco. *Della vita e delle opere di Girolamo Seripando.* Salerno: Raffaello Migliaccio, 1858.

Marranzini, Alfredo. "La figura del vescovo secondo Girolamo Seripando." *Una Hostia: Studi in onore del Cardinale Corrado Ursi.* Eds. Saturnino Muratore and Armando Rolla. Naples: M. D'Auria Editore, 1983.

Martin, John. *Venice's Hidden Enemies: Italian Heretics in a Renaissance City.* Berkeley: University of California Press, 1993.

McGinness, Frederick J. *Right Thinking and Sacred Oratory in Counter-Reformation Rome.* Princeton: Princeton University Press, 1995.

_____. "Preaching Ideals and Practice in Counter-Reformation Rome." *The Sixteenth Century Journal* 11 (1980): 109-127.

Menchi, Silvana Seidel. "Italy." *The Reformation in National Context.* Ed. Bob Scribner. Cambridge: Cambridge University Press, 1994.

Miele, Michele. "La penetrazione protestante a Salerno verso la metà del Cinquecento secondo un documento dell'Inquisizione." *Miscellanea Gilles Gerard Meersseman.* 2 vols. Padua: Editrice Antenore, 1970.

Moroni, Gaetano. *Dizionario di erudizione Storico-Ecclesiastico.* 109 vols. Venice: Emiliana, 1840-1879.

Olin, John C. *Six Essays on Erasmus.* New York: Fordham University Press, 1979.

O'Malley, John W. "Form, Content and Influence of Works About Preaching Before Trent: The Franciscan Contribution." *I Frati Minori tra '400 e '500: Atti del XII Convegno Internazionale, Assisi, 18-20 ottobre 1984.* Assisi: Centro di Studi Francescani, 1986.

_____. "Erasmus and the History of Sacred Rhetoric: The Ecclesiastes of 1535." *Erasmus of Rotterdam Society Yearbook* 5 (1985): 1-29.

_____. "Content and Rhetorical Forms in Sixteenth Century Treatises on Preaching." *Renaissance Eloquence: Studies in the Theory and Practice of Renaissance Rhetoric.* Ed. James J. Murphy. Berkeley: University of California Press, 1983.

_____. *Praise and Blame in Renaissance Rome.* Durham: Duke University Press, 1974.

Penna, Angelo. "Lo Studio della Bibbia nella spiritualità di S. Agostino." *Sanctus Augustinus Vitae Spiritualis Magister.* Rome: Analecta Augustiniana, 1959.

Perini, David A. *Bibliografia Augustiniana.* 3 vols. Florence: Artigianelli, 1935.

Petrocchi, Massimo. *Storia della Spiritualità Italiana.* 2 vols. Rome: Edizioni di Storia e Letteratura, 1978.

Ponticri, Ernesto. "Girolamo Seripando e la città di Salerno sua sede arcivescovile (1554-1563)." *Rassegna Storica Salernitana* 26 (1965): 3-28.

_____. "Figure e aspetti delle riforme cattolica-tridentina in Campania: Girolamo Seripando e Paolo Burali d'Arrezzo a Napoli." *Divagazioni Storiche e Storiografiche.* 2a serie. Naples: Libreria Scientifica, 1971.

_____. "La cultura umanistico-rinascimentale in Italia e la Chiesa Cattolica." *Divagazioni Storiche e Storiografiche.* 2a serie. Naples: Libreria Scientifica, 1971.

Pourrat, P. *Christian Spirituality.* 3 vols. London: Burns Oates and Washbourne, 1927.

Prosperi, Adriano. *Tra evangelismo e controriforma: G.M. Giberti.* Rome: Edizioni di storia e letteratura, 1969.

Rummel, Erika. *The Humanist-Scholastic Debate in the Renaissance and Reformation.* Cambridge: Harvard University Press, 1995.

Signorelli, Giuseppe. *Il Cardinale Egidio da Viterbo: Agostiniano, umanista e riformatore.* Florence: Editrice Fiorentina, 1929.

Stinger, Charles L. *The Renaissance in Rome.* Bloomington: Indiana University Press, 1985.

Taylor, Larissa. *Soldiers of Christ: Preaching in Late Medieval and Reformation France.* New York: Oxford University Press, 1992.

Tracy, James D. "Ad Fontes: The Humanist Understanding of Scripture as Nourishment for the Soul." *Christian Spirituality: High Middle Ages and Reformation.* Ed. Jill Raitt. New York: Crossroad, 1987.

Trapé, Agostino. "Il principio fondamentale della spiritualità Agostiniana e la vita monastica." *Sanctus Augustinus Vitae Spiritualis Magister.* Rome: Analecta Augustiniana, 1959.

van Luijk, Benigno A.L. *L'ordine Agostiniano e la Riforma monastica dal cinquecento alla vigilia della rivoluzione francese.* Louvain: Institut Historique Augustinien, 1973.

Weissman, Ronald F.E. "Sacred Eloquence: Humanist Preaching and Lay Piety in Renaissance Florence." *Christianity and the Renaissance: Image and Religious Imagination in the Quattrocento.* Eds. Timothy Verdon and John Henderson. Syracuse: Syracuse University Press, 1990.

Wright, A.D. *The Counter-Reformation: Catholic Europe and the Non-Christian World.* New York: St. Martin's Press, 1982.

Zizioulas, John D. "The Early Christian Community." *Christian Spirituality: Origins to the Twelfth Century.* Eds. Bernard McGinn, John Meyendorff, and Jean Leclercq. New York: Crossroad, 1985.

Zumkeller, Adolar. "The Spirituality of the Augustinians." *Christian Spirituality: High Middle Ages and Reformation.* Ed. Jill Raitt. New York: Crossroad, 1987.

# INDEX

abandonment:
    things of this world, 113-114
abbreviations, 17
abuse(-s), *See* reform...
Algranati, Gina, 19, 67n55
alms, 134
Ambrose, Saint, 78
Amulio, Marcantonio, Cardinal, 20
angels, 99
apologetics: bishops' duty, 80
Apostles:
    Apostles' Creed, 90, 95-96, 99, 117
    bishops and office of teaching, 75
Aquila (diocese), 36-37
Aragona, Giovanni d', 127, 128
Aristotle: *Organon*, 22
artists, 80-81
Augustine, Saint, 14, 21, 33, 47-48, 78, 83, 95, 99-100, 112, 113, 118, 156, 158
    on charity, 97-98
    piety, 54
    Platonism, 49
    rule of, 48
    on temptation, 107
Augustinians, 10, 14, 93, 156, 158
    *See also* prior general
    conditions (1551), 30
    external reform, 28
    general chapter (1507), 22
    general chapter (1539), 27
    general chapter (1547; Recanati), 35
    general chapter; Lombard congregation, 35
    learning and piety, 49
    pomp in general chapters, 28
    Protestantism within, 26-27
    reform, 24, 27, 48
    reform statutes, 29, 30
    renewal of studies, 28
    serious problems (1549), 35
    Seripando as reformer, 155
    spirituality, 50-51
    traditional studies, 21
    uniformity, 29
    visitations by Seripando, 28-30
    visitations: Umbria and Lazio, 35
Averroists, 49

Bagnoli, Ambrogio Salvio da, 61, 63
baptism, 109
    become member of Christ's body, 108
    bless day of sencond birth, 108
    cursing our first birth, 108
    dead to sin, 108
    faith and the sponsor, 32
    foundation for renewal, 109
    sign of faith, 106-107
    washed clean from sin in, 106
barons, 20
Basil, Saint, 78
beliefs: preaching, 93
Benedictine nuns, 126
benefices, 77, 128, 131, 145, 148
Bergamo, 73
bible, 54, 118

centrality of, 133-134
daily reading, 100, 101
errors; Seripando at Council of Trent, 31
food for the soul, 100
infallible truth, 100
meditating on, 80
sense of, 94
reading; Council of Trent, 32, 33
sermons and, 99-101
spiritual formation, 99, 113
understanding God's word, 95, 100

bishop (-s):
   See also diocese; episcopacy; residence
   bishop (the word), 79
   characteristics (ideal), 77
   defending teachings of the Church, 80
   demeanor, 81
   church; sixteenth century, 155
   eucharistic assembly, 111
   example; early church, 78, 81
   faith in prayers of the people, 77
   the faithful as his children, 83
   faults in appointment of, 72
   humble, generous, unselfish ministry, 85
   leadership, 79
   learning by, 80
   model, 10
   neglect of responsibilities, 73, 155
   nonresidence in Salerno, 59
   nonresidence in their dioceses, 70
   office of teaching, 75
   overseer, 79
   pastoral ministry, 72, 74, 75
   pastoral obligations, 40-41, 91
   pastoral office, 82, 91
   pastoral reform by, 157
   patristic age, 14, 157
   practices in appointment of, 70
   preaching as duty of, 31m 73, 79, 90, 91, 94, 134, 156
   principal duties, 73
   reform-minded; example, 25
   relations with their clergy, 73
   religious orders; Council of Trent, 31-32
   residing in Rome, 40
   responsibility of a father, 84-85
   restoration of office of, 13-14
   role and functions of, 150
   ship's steersman (metaphor), 85

spiritual bond with the faithful, 77
teacher, pastor, father, 79, 80, 83
teaching by word and example, 81, 82
teaching effectiveness, 80
temporal interests, 77
virtues proper to, 73-74
works of, 82

Bologna, 23, 35
books: forbidden, 61
Borda, Mattia, 146
Borromeo, Charles, 71, 158
bread:
   See also eucharist; panem
   third bread mentioned in scripture, 111

canons (cathedral chapter), 144-146
Capograsso, Domenico, 76
Carafa, Mario, 61, 62
cardinals, 39
catechesis: sermons, 95-97
catechism schools, 115
cathedral:
   chapter: functions and privileges, 144
   sermon on dedication of, 90
Catholic Church:
   See also Church; Council of Trent; Reformation
   internal renewal needed, 40
Cervantes, Gaspare, 147
Cesareo, Francesco C., 15
charities, 55
charity:
   See also love
   Augustine on, 97-98
   bringing back those gone astray, 39
   inner worship, 103
   perfection and, 98, 99
   sermon theme, 97-99
   sign of remission of sin, 105
   works of, 99
Charles V, Emperor, 24, 25, 36, 37, 38, 56, 61, 69, 129
children: sermons to, 115-118
chrism, 107
Christian life, 109, 134
   Christ living in us, 113
   eucharist as center of, 111
   ever-deepening, 114
   godparents' duty, 117
   Lord's Prayer, 96
   renewal, 95, 98, 99, 115-116
   sermons and building up, 91, 156
Christianity:

# Index

charity in, 97
humanism and, 53
permeating daily life, 91
Platonism and, 50
Christians:
    apostolic communities (early), 55
    equality, 102
    reading pagan authors, 52
Christopher of Padua, 93
Church:
    See also bishops; clergy; episcopacy
    abuses and problems in, 139
    apostolic ideal, 125
    body formed in, 111
    body; members, 109
    Christians living in community, 109
    desire that it be very poor and very holy, 125
    eucharistic assembly, 111
    holiness, 136-138, 157
    honored by individual merits, 19
    hope for reform, 64
    laity; holiness, 137-138
    one body, one head, 139
    power to forgive sins, 104
    regeneration, 55
    renewal, 47
    unity, 118, 138, 139
    visible head willed by Christ, 42
church buildings: deterioration, 129
church history: four ages, 125
church property, 145
Cicero, 49, 52, 53
classical learning, 65n23
classical literature, 51
Clement VII, Pope, 25
clergy (*especially reform program*):
    absence from diocese, 135
    abuses, 38
    behavior, 135
    benefices, 131, 132, 145, 148
    concubinage, 131, 135
    constitutions (1484) on life of, 127-128
    correction of customs of, 72
    cultural formation, 132
    education, 132
    example, 134-135
    exempt, 128, 141, 147
    garb, 131
    holiness of the Church, 136
    honest living, 141
    key to diocesan reform, 142, 143
    liturgy, 134
    Mass, 136
    moral failures, 78
    motivation of priests in Salerno, 130
    ordination and first Mass, 133
    personal acquaintance with, 132
    personal reform, 131
    preaching, 134
    proper formation, 55, 60
    relations with their bishops, 73
    residency, 135, 157
    revival of spiritual life, 64
    secular lifestyle, 60
    synod (1554), 130-136
    way of life, 149
    worthiness to celebrate Mass, 136
Cocciano, Augusto, 35, 75, 127, 129, 131
Cochlaeus, Johann, 23
Coduto, Prospero, 58
commandments, 117, 130
common good, 98
communion, holy, See eucharist
community, 109-110
    eucharist and building up, 110
    Lord's Prayer, 109
    social beings, 109
    unity of the Spirit, 110
concubinage, 131
concupiscence, 32-33
confession:
    constitutions (1554), 130
    monetary penances, 133
    positive effects, 105
    practice of postponing, 104-105
    priests celebrating Mass, 136
    regularity, 138
    written license to hear, 133
confessors, 133
confraternities, 101-102, 149
conscience:
    examination of, 136
    obligation of residency, 40
*Consilium de emendanda ecclesia*, 74
Contarini, Gasparo, 73-74, 75
contemplation, 54-55
    ascent of the soul to God, 49
    life of action from, 98
contrition, 105, 136
conversion:
    change in the soul, 105
    penitential spirit, 105
    reformers' call for, 47
    sign of remission of sin, 105
corporal works of mercy, 98-99, 135
Council of Trent, 9, 14, 19, 30, 71, 72, 73, 85, 92, 94, 148, 157
    bishops and religious orders, 31-32
    disciplinary reform, 34

episcopal office, 155
  first period, 30-35
  Lutheranism and, 31
  problems in Bologna, 35
  on reading the bible, 32, 33
  reform decrees, 150
  reform movements, 13
  renewal of the Church as aim, 31
  Seripando as papal legate, 39-42
  third period (1561) opened, 40
  transferred to Bologna, 35
creation: eschatological end, 111
creatures: dependence on, 33
Creed, 80, 103
  *See also* Apostles
cross, 102
  *Cum sicut accepimus*, 146

damnation, 108
dancing, 135
Dardano, Matteo, 58
deacons, 111
death, 112, 114, 137
dependence: on creatures, 33-34
desecularization, 27
desire:
  highest good: return to God, 114
  union with God, 114
devil, 107, 117
devotion, 47, 114
*De baptismo et confirmatione*, 34
*De peccato originale*, 32
*De sacramentis*, 34
dignity, 82, 101, 126
dioceses:
  neglect in, 72-73
  personal governing by bishop, 34, 39
discrimination, 109
Divine Office, 137
Dominicans, 21

early church, 137, 150, 157, 158
  ministry of the Word, 83
  pastoral duties, 125
Eboli (Benedictine nuns), 126
Eck, Johann, 23
education:
  catechetical lessons, 118
  children of Salerno, 115
  Christian ethics, 116
  humanism, 51
episcopacy, 69-88
  *See also* bishop
  image in early Church Fathers, 78
  model, 158
  office of service, not honor, 79

Pacheco on reform of, 71
pastoral aspect, 34, 39, 40
Paul on, 77, 81
Peter's office, 82
reforms; sixteenth century, 155
renewal of the Church, 34
seeking the honor of, 77
Seripando's understanding of, 75-85
spiritual nature of the office, 71
state of, 70-74
Erasmus, 52
  on petition in prayer, 102
  on preaching, 92, 94
eschatology: eucharistic mystery, 111
Espence, Claude d', 40
Estella, Diego de, 93-94
eternal life, 113
  eucharist and, 112
  realized through communion, 111
ethics: Christian education, 116
eucharist, 109, 110-113
  *See also: panem*
  building up Christian community, 110
  crucial for spiritual life, 111
  daily reception, 113
  effects; eternal life, 112
  eschatological messianic community, 111
  frequent reception of communion, 123n115, 134, 138
  heretical teachings, 111
  medicine, 112
  mystical meal, 112
  ontological context, 112
  real presence, 62
  salvation and eternal life, 111, 136
  spiritual life; three elements, 112-113
  spiritual well-being, 135, 136
  taken to home of the sick, 137
  unifying Christians into community, 111
  worthiness always to receive, 113
Europe, 11, 70, 53, 59, 92, 97
evangelical counsels, 102, 103
evangelism, 55
evangelization, 24
*Exigit tuae*, 141
example, 134-135, 138
  children corrupted by, 117
  good behavior; effect, 81, 82
excommunication, 133, 139, 140

faith, 33-34, 93, 96, 117
    abandoning, 138-139
    baptism as sign of, 106-107
    inner worship, 103
    justifies when one with love, 34
    prayer and, 78
    remission of original sin, 32
    sign of remission of sin, 105
    Trinity, 51
fall of man: effects, 50
false testimony, 81
Farnese, Alessandro, 24-25
fasting, 134, 135
Fathers of the Church:
    image of bishops, 78
    prayers of petition, 102
    sermons, 93, 156
Fava, Antonio, 19, 67n55
Ficino, Marsilio, 49-50
Flaminio, Marcantonio, 114
food: carnal and spiritual, 112
forgiveness of sin:
    certainty of, 105
    grant us today..., 104
    prayer and, 33
    signs of remission, 105
forgiving others:
    admonishing in sermons, 134
free will: grace and spiritual life, 50
Fregoso, Federico, 72, 142
friars, 53-54, 145, 146

Gabriele (schoolteacher), 115
Galeota, Isabella, 20
Giberti, Gianmatteo, 25, 34, 74, 75, 158
Giles of Rome, 48
Giles of Viterbo, 10, 11, 22, 48
Giovanni Antonio (prior general), 26
God:
    dependence on, 33
    goal of all humanity, 114
    healing and redeeming, 33
    knowing, by the soul, 114
    majesty of, 92
godfathers: number permitted, 127
godparents, 117, 138
Gonzaga, Cardinal, 40
good works, 33, 34, 50, 94, 99, 112, 113
goodness:
    infinite, 53
    will of God, 51
gospel, 134, 158
    bread of life, 100
    focus of preaching, 80
grace, 27, 33, 80, 137
    cooperating with, 93
    prayer and, 33
    primacy of, 50
    salvific work of Christ, 107
Granvella (chancellor), 38, 69
Greco, Orazio, 142-143
greed, 110, 137
Greek language, 22
Greek literature, 49, 52
Guerrero, Archbishop, 40

happiness, 113, 114
heart, 93, 96, 118
    prayer from, 54, 55
    purification, 111
hedonism, 117
Henry II, King of France, 56
heresy, 60, 61, 127, 138, 139
    synod of 1554, 63-64
holidays, religious, 127
holiness, 132, 136
    laity and, 137-138
Holy Orders:
    draft of decree, 42
    prescriptions for candidates, 132
holy places, 137
Holy Spirit, 32, 82
    fruits of, 112
    gifts; members of the Church, 109
    preaching and, 134
hope, 33-34
    inner worship, 103
    Trinity, 51
human nature:
    corruption of, 107
    desires of the flesh and, 108
humanism (-ists), 10, 24, 48, 89-90, 100, 102, 156
    *See also* Renaissance
    Christian, 52-53
    description, 11
    intellectual movement, 56
    monks, friars, and scholarship, 53-54
    scholasticism and, 65n23
    service of the Church, 52
    the term, 51, 52
    theological problems, 52, 53
    vehicle for reform, 54
humans: social beings, 109
Hutten, Ulrich von, 23
hypocrites, 80-81, 138

ideas: Platonic theory, 50
Ignatius of Antioch, Saint, 111, 112
ignorance, 52, 131, 143
illitracy, 93
image of God:
    participation in salvation, 93

imperfection, 33
individual(-s; ism), 54, 111
Inquisition, 39, 61, 62, 63
intellect, 55, 89
    educating, 53
    intellectual life, 63
    subjugate to Christ, 100
Italy, 23, 53, 59, 70, 90, 92, 94, 97, 101, 115, 138

Jedin, Hubert, 13, 19, 32, 49, 67n55, 86n12
Jerome, Saint, 78
Jesus Christ, 81, 85, 110, 117, 137
    *See also* redemption
    abandonment to, 103
    cornerstone of Christian community, 110
    corporal works of mercy, 98-99
    imitation of Christ, 102
    invisible head of the Church, 42
    primacy of, 50
    real presence in the Mass, 111
    resurrection; new life, 33
    reverence at Mass, 134
    sharing in sonship of, 109
    subjugate intellect to, 100
    time spent in preaching, 79
John Carroll University, 15
John Chrysostom, Saint, 78
jokes, 137
Joranko, Sally, 15
joy, 100
Julius III, Pope, 19, 37, 128
justice, 29, 94, 97, 99
justification, 25, 48
    Augustinian understanding of, 33
    Council of Trent, 32
    movement proceeding from God, 33
    primal; act of God, 34
    three things necessary for, 33-34

Kelly, Joseph F., 14
Knapp, Caron, 15
Kristeller, 51

laity, 54, 78, 91, 95
    holiness in the Church, 137-138
    inner spiritual life, 138
    lay piety, 101-103
    progress in prayer, 102
    reform of, 136-139
    self denial, 102
    social virtues, 101
language: *humanitas*, 52
Lateran Council, 4th, 123n115

Lateran Council, 5th, 70
Latin literature, 51-52
laughter, 137
law: charity as perfection of, 98
Lazio, 35
leadership, 79
lead: condition of contemporary Church, 125
Lent, 23
liberal education, 51
Lippomano, Pietro, 73
liturgical life, 27, 28, 130, 137
logic, 52
Longo, Francesco, 148
Lord's Prayer, 80, 81, 90, 95-96, 98, 117
    daily bread, 101
    forgive us our trespasses, 106
    give us this day, 100
    hallowed be thy name, 99
    *Oratione Fraterna*, 109
    petitions, 96, 102
    sermons on, 102, 103
    sermons to children, 115
love, 27, 33-34, 55
    *See also* charity
    bishops motivated by, 83, 85
    Christ's command, 98
    faith and justification, 34
    most in need, 99
    movement toward God, 98
    of neighbor, 98
    primacy of, 50
    Trinity, 51
Luis de Granada, 94
Luther, Martin, 9, 10, 25, 26, 31, 47, 59
Lutheranism, 26-27, 31, 61, 139

Mary, Blessed Virgin, 134
Mary Magdalene, 105
Mass, 41-42, 138
    constitutions (1554), 130
    disorder, 137
    license to celebrate, 136
    real presence of Christ, 111
    reverence, 134, 135
    synod (1554), 136
Matins, 22
Matthew, Saint: relics, 75, 91
Matthew (gospel) 16:24, 102
Maximus the Confessor, 111
McManamon, John, S.J., 14
merit:
    gift of God, 50
    honor of the Catholic Church, 19
middle ages, 56
Milan, 61

Milensius, Felix, 20
modesty, 135, 137
monastic communities (nuns), 42, 126
    chaplain, 140
    confessional, 141
    constitutions (1554), 130
    enclosure, 140
    gifts or letters, 141
    grate, 140
    license to go outside monastery, 140
    poverty; work, 140
    reform of, 140
    sacristy, 140
monasticism:
    communal life, 27-28
    reform fundamentals, 30
money, 137
monks: humanism, 53-54
moral education, 55
moral life, 100, 112, 137
    cleansing; knowing God, 114
    concupiscence, 33
    worthy always to receive Christ, 113
mortification, 94
mystical body, 109-110
    unity as sign of, 139
mysticism, 49, 50, 111, 112

Naples, 20, 22, 35, 38, 48, 55, 61, 63, 69, 76
natural philosophy, 49
neighbor: service of love, 98, 110
Neoplatonism, 21, 49-50
nobility:
    episcopal appointments, 72
    merchant class, 58
    Neapolitan, 20, 37
    privileges, 57
    wealth, 57
nuns, *See* monastic communities (nuns)

obedience, 100
Olin, John C., 9-11
oratory, 53, 92
Oratory of Divine Love, 25
Order of Saint Clare, 126
original sin, 53
    Council of Trent, 32-33

Pacheco, Cardinal, 38, 69, 71
pagan authors, 52
Paleotti, Gabriele, 158
pallium:
    archiepiscopal authority, 38, 70

*panem*:
    bread of tears, 103-104
    Lord's Prayer, 100, 101
papacy: Seripando at the Council of Trent, 42
parents, 84, 138
    religious teaching of children, 117
    teaching need to be penitent, 106
parishes: religious beneficiaries, 148
Patavino, Ambrogio, 21
Paul, Saint, 31, 50, 109, 118, 133, 156, 157
    Acts 20:28, 41
Paul III, Pope, 24-25, 26, 30, 35, 74, 147
Paul IV, Pope, 70, 141
Paul of Genazzano, 22
peace, 27
penance (sacrament), 34-35
    *See also* confession; repentance
    need to receive, 104, 105, 106
    Protestant teaching; errors, 35
    reform of administration of, 133
penances: monetary, 133
perfection, 51, 102, 103, 113
    charity and, 98, 99
    Christian, 97
    love and, 50
    temptation and, 107, 108
personality: humanist spirituality, 54
persuasion: sermons, 92, 93
Peter, Saint, Apostle, 82, 104
philology, 52
philosophy, 21, 23
Piedmont, 61
piety, 94, 95, 117, 149
    abuses, 63
    biblically based, 101
    humanist concerns (three), 54
Pius IV, Pope, 39, 41, 146, 147, 148, 150
Placito di Sangro, 51
Plato, 48, 49
Platonism, 21, 24
Pomponazzo, Pietro, 23
Pontian Academy, 48, 49
poor and rich, 97
popes:
    primacy, 41, 71
    role in reform of the Church, 43
    visible head of the Church, 42
Posilipo, 35
prayer, 82, 96, 102
    bishop and his people, 77
    faith and, 78
    heart or ritual, 54
    perfection through, 103

petition only as in Lord's Prayer, 102
progress and stages in, 102
weapon against temptation, 106
preach(-ers; -ing), 23
*See also* sermons
Apostolic See and, 31
bishops, early Church, 83
classical oratory, 92
effective preachers, 21-22, 91
Erasmus on, 92, 94
fifty words, 134
gospel as focus of, 80
humanist, 53
obligation, 134
pastoral duty, 96
pray for good preachers, 83
principal aim of, 118, 156
principal duty of bishops, 31, 73, 79, 80, 156
religious instruction in, 32, 79, 90, 91
rights of religious, 31-32
Seripando admired for, 23-24
Seripando's reform program, 119
sixteenth century styles, 92-94
teaching; moving; delight, 92
Tridentine legislation, 91, 94
vehicle of reform, 24
predestination, 48
priests:
*See also* clergy
confession before Mass, 136
formation, 131-132
primitivism, 125
prior general:
personal influence, 28
qualifications for administration, 27
Protestantism, 60, 63
within the Augustinians, 26-27
punishment, 93
for holding Lutheran views, 27
purification, 119
purity, 99

qualifications:
for administering a community, 27
for ordination, 132
Quignones, Francesco, Cardinal, 31

rationalists, 80-81
reason(-ing), 52, 90
redemption, 32, 53
restoration to grace, 107
reform (Seripando's program), 20, 75, 76, 115, 118, 125-153, 157

*See also* Augustinians; clergy; episcopacy; residency
Augustinian Order, 27
beginning with the individual, 29, 30
benefices, 145, 148
chapter accepts constitutions, 147
children and, 116
continued from Council of Trent, 30
directives, reproaches, advice, 30
eligibility for canonry, 144-145
lifelong concern, 42-43
Neapolitan humanists, 55
obstacles to, 143-149
pastoral visitation, 141-143
persuasion mode, 29
preaching in, 89
Seripando's understanding of, 27
sermons in, 29, 156
summary of, 149-150
traditional privileges, 144
word and example, 28
Reformation (in the Catholic Church), 19, 25, 158
*See also* bishops; clergy; preaching
Augustinians as advocates of, 21
bishop as pastor and teacher, 77
bishops and regulars, 48
conditions crying out for, 40
efforts prior to Luther, 9
humanism and, 11
office of bishop, 13
pope's essential role in, 43
pre-Lutheran origin, 47
pre-Tridentine, 155
restored episcopacy as key to, 155, 158
Seripando's episcopacy, 14
sixteenth century, 9-10, 125
Tridentine, 13
Reformation, Protestant:
common origin with Catholic reformation, 47
emphases, 48
reform movement, 63, 64
religious conditions:
Church in decline, 78
mercenaries, 77
religious instruction:
role of bishops; sermons, 79, 84, 90, 92
religious life:
vows = denial of self, 102
religious orders:
Augustinian Rule, 48
Council of Trent, 31-32
humanism, 54

## Index

reform, 42
  sixteenth century formations, 10
  visiting and reforming, 147-148
religious revival:
  institutional and personal, 47
renewal:
  inner, *See* spiritual life.
  post-Reformation Catholic efforts, 9, 40
Renaissance, 10, 20, 47, 49, 54, 92, 94, 115
  humanism, 51-55
  new learning, 56
  religious orders, 54
  rhetorical culture, 52
  scholasticism and, 52-53
repentance, 94, 97, 136
  bread of tears, 103-104
  gift from God, 104
  sign of remission of sin, 105
  signs of penitence, 106
  spirit of penitence, 130
  true, 103-104
residency (bishops and clergy), 34, 41, 71, 72, 74, 75, 77, 86n12, 135, 142, 156, 157
  Council of Trent, 40, 41, 70, 71, 157
  divine law, 34, 40, 41, 71
  non-residence as norm, 10, 70
  visitations, 24, 39, 156
revelation: Platonism and, 50
revenues: collecting; vicars, 70
reward, 93
rhetoric, 53, 92
rich and poor, 97
Ridolfi, Nicolo, 72, 142
Roman classics, 49
Roman Curia, 141
Rome, 29, 31, 35, 70, 75
  number of bishops residing in, 40
Rotelle, John E., O.S.A., 15
Rummel, Erika, 65n23

sacraments, 55, 80, 137, 138, 139
Saint Augustine (monastery in Salerno), 69
saints, 135, 138
Salerno (diocese), 19
  brief allowing Seripando to take possession of, 70
  cathedral, 72
  cathedral chapter, 76, 128-129, 143-146
  cathedral in ruins, 129
  clerical income low, 126
  conditions in, 14, 126-128
  constitutions (1554), 130
  disrepair and ruin in, 127, 129
  economic poverty, 126, 127, 129
  economic improvement, 58
  faith life, 60
  heretical teachings in, 60
  monastic communities, 126
  nonresident bishops, 59, 72, 142, 156
  pastoral visitation, 39, 141-143
  positive picture, 143
  reform program, 118, 125-153
  Seripando's sermons, 90-92
  spiritual life, 144
  spiritual ruins, 129
  summary of Seripando's role, 10, 150
  synod (1554), 39, 63, 128, 129
  synodal constitutions (1484), 127-128
  urban and rural priests, 131
  vicars caring for, 142
Salerno (the place), 34, 49, 55-64, 95, 110
  academic institutions, 57
  class warfare, 58, 110
  cultural climate, 56, 57, 60
  economic problems, 58, 129
  educational institutions, 85
  intellectual influences, 64
  new religious ideas in, 63
  nobility, 57
  population, 55
  religious problems, 59
  social conditions, 97
  trade center, 56
  university faculties in, 63
  worldly values, 59
  youth of, 116
salvation, 47, 101, 116, 138, 142
  bishops' work, 84, 94
  eucharist and, 136
  realized through communion, 111
San Giacomo in Bologna (monastery), 23
San Giovanni a Carbonara (monastery), 21, 24, 37
Sanseverino, Ferrante, 56, 57, 60, 63, 84, 110, 126, 129, 131
Santa Caterina a Formello (monastery), 21
Sant'Agostino in Siena (monastery), 23
Savonarola, 9
scandal, 128
schismatics, 127
scholastic curriculum, 51
scholasticism, 52, 65n23
schools: motivation for, 116

Sciabica, Girolamo, 148
scriptures, *See* bible
sects, 139
secularism, 28, 117
self denial, 102
self-righteousness, 50
Seripando, Ferrante, 20
Seripando, Francesco, 21
Seripando, Girolamo
   *See also* Augustinians; Council of Trent
   archbishop of Salerno, 38-39
   Augustinian vocation, 22
   biography, 19-46
   birth date and place, 20
   cardinalate, 39
   career, 9
   classical knowledge, 49
   consecrated bishop (1554), 38
   contemplative bent, 48
   death of, 42, 147, 148
   diary, 21
   early life, 20-22
   early years as an Augustinian, 22-26
   economic concerns, 84, 129
   education (early), 21, 22
   episcopal renewal (his example), 85
   exempt religious and, 147-148
   father of his diocese, 84, 85
   formation of priests, 131-132
   governed diocese while at Trent, 149
   governing the Augustinian Order, 24
   health, 35, 36, 38, 42
   historical context of his life, 13
   intellectual formation, 22
   intellectual/political world of, 47-68
   lector, 22
   legate to Council of Trent, 39-42, 76, 148
   library founded by, 37
   master of studies (1518), 22, 23
   name change, 21
   Neapolitan nobility (ambassador), 37
   nominated as bishop of Aquila, 36, 38, 69
   nominated as bishop of Salerno, 69
   pastor and teacher, 85
   personal acquaintance with his clergy, 132
   piety of, 50-51
   Platonist, 48
   preaching admired, 23-24
   preparing for death, 37
   presence among his people, 83, 149
   principal activities, 24
   prior general (1539-1551), 26-30, 36
   promise never to be absent from diocese, 75
   reform of episcopal office, 155
   refuge in Benedictine monastery, 57
   regent and master (1519), 23
   register, 22
   religious vocation, 21
   residency observed, 75-76
   scriptor (appointment), 22
   sermons (analysis) *See* sermons.
   significance of, 157
   spiritual teachings, 89-123
   Tridentine bishop, 157
   vicar general, 24
   works: *De ingressu ad episcopatum*, 78
   years following the Council, 35-38
Seripando, Marcello, 148-149
sermons (general and teachings of Seripando), 29
   *See also* preaching
   aim, 24
   Augustinian spirituality, 14
   Bible and, 99-101
   catechetical, 91, 95-97
   charity (theme), 97-99
   children of Salerno, 115-118
   directives, 93
   emphases, 118
   explanation of the gospel, 134
   humanist preachers, 53
   intellect addressed in, 89-90
   medieval scholastic, 92
   moral tone, 92
   Pauline letters; receiving Christ, 90
   penitential, 94
   persuasion, 92, 93
   Protestant message in, 61
   religious formation through, 79
   responsibility, 10
   scripture used in, 90, 118
   simple language, 93
   spiritual renewal as focus, 156
   spiritual teachings in, 89-123
   style and content, 89, 94
   teaching doctrine through, 119
   understanding God's word, 90
   Word of God bearing fruit, 99

Sessa (monastery), 22
sick, 112, 135
Simonetta, Cardinal, 41
sin:
    baptism = death to sin, 108
    carnal life, 113
    concupiscence, 33
    cursing one's first birth, 107-108
    *See* forgiveness of sin.
    heart of stone, 105
    justification, 33
    sorrow; bread of tears, 103-104
Sirleto, Guglielmo, 78
social classes, 95, 110
solitude, 38
Solofra: visitation in, 143
sophists, 80-81
Sorrento, 23
soul:
    divine, 114
    immortality, 49
    knowledge of God, 114
spiritual life, 28, 55, 94, 97
    Augustinian, 99
    Bible and formation, 99
    biblical approach to, 111
    bread (scripture) needed for, 100
    catechetical lessons, 118
    charity as soul of, 97
    Christocentric, 107
    dying to self, 113
    ecclesial experience, 109
    end = union with God, 114
    eucharist; three elements, 111, 112-113
    goal: renewal of Christian society, 54
    grace and free will, 50
    gradations; perfection, 101
    humanist, 97
    inner renewal, 14, 99, 100, 101, 115, 157, 158
    laity, 138
    relational aspect; community, 109
    revival, 64
    teaching of Ignatius of Antioch, 111
    *See* union with God.
    walking toward God, 114
    worldliness and, 113-114
sponsors at baptism, 32
study, 28, 37
superiors: qualifications for, 27
synod:
    guidelines for, 38-39, 128
    preaching, 134
    results, 141

tears: sign of remission of sin, 105
temporal goods, 27
    bishops' concern for, 85
temptation, 78
    battle against, 106
    faith, 138-139
    opportunity to praise God, 107
    perfection; strength, 107, 108
Ten Commandments, 80
textual criticism, 52
Theatines, 61
theatre, 135
theologians:
    scholastic method, 52, 53
    task: reforming people's lives, 53
theology, 21, 23, 27
    Christocentric, 107
    humanism, 53
    pastoral, 91
    Platonic, 89
    practical concerns, 91
Thomas Aquinas, Saint, 48
Thomas of Villanova, Saint, 10
Toledo, 56
Toledo, Pietro di, 37, 63
Tolliero, Don Pietro, 146
Tomas de Herrera, 19
Torres, Ludovico de, 38, 69, 72, 142
traditionalists, 80-81
Trent, *See* Council of Trent
Trinity, 51, 112
truth, 81, 100, 101
Turks, 57, 58, 127

Umbria, 35
union with God, 100, 113-115
    divine initiative, 114
    inner renewal, 115
unity: Christian community, 110

Valdes, Juan de, 61
Valencia, 10
values, 118
Venice, 60, 61
Vera, Giovanni de, 72
Verona, 34, 74
viaticum, 137
vicar general, 144
vicars, 70
    pastoral visitations by, 72
vice, 92-93, 94, 127
Villamarino, Isabella, 56, 62, 63
Virgil, 49
virtue(-s), 33, 92-93, 94, 112
    bishops, 73-74
visitations, 24, 39, 72
    Augustinians, 28-29

religious, economic, moral conditions, 29
Seripando's letter (24 Oct 1557), 142
vocation: call to justification, 33
voluntarism, 51
vows: religious life, 102

will, 53, 118
will of God, 51, 96, 99, 112, 113
worldliness, 59
    abandoning things of this world, 113-114
    youth of Salerno, 116-117
worship, 103, 137
wrongdoing: bishops offending their flocks, 82

Ximenes, Cardinal, 9

youth of Salerno, 55, 149

Zorilla, Alfonso, 93